D0462631

Design: Caroline King

Maps & Mapping: Bartholomew Mapping, a division of HarperCollins, Glasgow

Printing: Canale, Italy

UK Distribution: Portfolio, Greenford, Middlesex

US Distribution: The Globe Pequot Press, Guilford, Connecticut

Published in February 2003

Alastair Sawday Publishing Co. Ltd
The Home Farm Stables, Barrow Gurney, Bristol BS48 3RW
Tel: +44 (0)1275 464891 Fax: +44 (0)1275 464887
E-mail: info@specialplacestostay.com Web: www. specialplacestostay.com

The Globe Pequot Press
P. O. Box 480, Guilford, Connecticut 06437, USA
Tel: +1 203 458 4500 Fax: +1 203 458 4601
E-mail: info@globe-pequot.com Web: www.globe-pequot.com

Fourth edition

Copyright © January 2003 Alastair Sawday Publishing Co. Ltd

ISBN 1-901970- 60-4 in the UK
ISBN 0-7627-2550-8 in the US

Printed in Italy

ALASTAIR SAWDAY'S
SPECIAL PLACES TO STAY

PARIS
HOTELS

The
Globe
Pequot
Press

Guilford
Connecticut, USA

ALASTAIR
SAWDAY
PUBLISHING

Alastair Sawday Publishing
Bristol, UK

EDITED BY ANN COOKE-YARBOROUGH

CONTENTS

Acknowledgements • A word from Alastair Sawday

Introduction • General map • Maps • Metro map

CONTENTS

CONTENTS

CONTENTS

See the back of the book for:
- Useful vocabulary • Making the most of Paris
- Introduction to French furniture
- Other Special Places to Stay titles
- What is Alastair Sawday Publishing? • Essential reading
- ww.specialplacestostay.com • Book order form • Report form
- Quick reference indices • Index • Exchange rate table
- Guide to our symbols •

ACKNOWLEDGEMENTS

Ann Cooke-Yarborough needs no introduction to the thousands of travellers who have used this superb little book for years. She's the original 'trooper'. She is asked to do it, and she does it – without a murmur of worry or complaint. Heaven only knows (I'd rather not) what goes on behind the scenes but the results are always the same: dependable, inspired and inspiring. This book buzzes with her very individual approach to life – and to hotels. She can spot a fraud a kilometre away, sniff out a pretender and detect any lapse in taste. But, more importantly, she knows an authentic enthusiast when she sees one. Her selection of hotels is awash with fascinating people who have made real commitments to their hotels and to the people who sleep in them. It takes an interesting woman with high standards to acknowledge the same qualities in others. We are all grateful to her.

I must, too, acknowledge her support system – Brendan Flanagan, whose tolerance knows few limits. I suspect that he does more to help than either of them will admit. Thank you, both of you.

Alastair Sawday

Series Editor:	Alastair Sawday
Editor:	Ann Cooke-Yarborough
Editorial Director:	Annie Shillito
Production Manager:	Julia Richardson
Web Producer:	Russell Wilkinson
Production Assistants:	Rachel Coe, Paul Groom
Editorial Assistants:	Jo Boissevain, Roanne Finch
Accounts:	Jenny Purdy
Marketing:	Paula Brown, Bryony Johnstone
PR:	Sarah Bolton
Title page illustrations:	Aymeric Chastnenet
Furniture drawings:	Mathias Fournier

A WORD FROM
ALASTAIR SAWDAY

There is – still – little to compare with the sheer man-made beauty of Paris. You may be impressed by Budapest, agape at Prague or awe-struck in Manhattan – but in Paris you are, somehow, special. Or you are part of a show that is especially, beautiful. Those unforgettable black-and-white photos by Cartier-Bresson – a couple kissing on a bridge, an old man on a bicycle – don't seem like archive material at all. Paris is authentically itself, unchanged, however modern in (well-publicised) parts. Yet one of its greatest assets is, still, its ability to astonish, to be architecturally brave, to cock a snook. Wandering the streets, rapt, you will turn a corner and have your eyebrows lifted. The old magic is there but there is new magic, too – generated, for example, by modern buildings such as the Pompidou Centre and the Louvre pyramids.

A word about our new cover design: we hope that it is fresher and more contemporary than those lovely watercolours – which we are sad to lose. They have always set us apart but we feel that our style is now well-entrenched and respected and we are free to branch out with a new design.

We have always said that 'a night in Paris is too precious to be spent in the wrong hotel'. It remains true, and Ann Cooke-Yarborough's book is as valuable a resource as ever – awash with wise suggestions and elegant descriptions. Picture, if you will, a redoubtable English woman striding purposefully through the streets of Paris, in all weathers, in pursuit of her ideal hotel. She does it on your behalf and saves you hours of disappointment – and tramping of streets. The result is a near certain knowledge on your part that a trusted friend with a sympathetic feel for what it is you are looking for has gone on ahead of you and has reported back – with panache, style and acuity.

A clever parent, according to Harry Truman (sic!), finds out what the children want and then advises them to do it. Those in 'business' are often told to do the same for their clients. We break the rules and do the opposite: we find what we like and then tell you about it. But it works a treat.

Here is lots more of what we, and especially Ann, like. May Paris do for you what it has done for generations of its admirers

Alastair Sawday

INTRODUCTION

Paris city A new broom has been sweeping the streets of Paris since we
elected a radically new green-leaning city council in 2001.
The dog mess problem (16 tonnes a day) has visibly improved
since fines have been levied and seen to be levied. Rubbish is
collected and the streets of Paris cleaned every single day and
waste sorting – paper, packaging and household gadgets, glass,
rubbish – is now mandatory in all residential areas. It remains
to educate the population about the real advantages of recycling.

More effort is being made to reduce air pollution by
discouraging private cars and promoting public transport:

* residents' parking is cheaper and easier; occasional parking
  has become very expensive;

* growing miles of dedicated bus lanes are making surface
  public transport faster and more attractive – there's no better
  way to do a tour of the city than on certain bus routes – and
  off-peak trains are more frequent on the metro (already at its
  maximum at peak hours). As always, we urge you not to use
  your car in Paris – garage it as soon as you arrive or, better
  still, don't bring it at all.

Paris hotels Ideas to make the city more festive and fun for residents and
visitors alike are being tried out. Paris Plage, the 'beach' along
the Seine – sand, parasols, deck chairs and ice cream stalls on
the normally traffic-maddened expressway – was a great success
in July and August 2002, producing lots of goodwill and gentle
holiday fun, such rarities in our sophisticated city, and will
be repeated in 2003, bigger and better but possibly not yet
with donkey rides (they are still offered for children in the
Luxembourg Gardens). In winter, three free municipal skating
rinks are set up where anyone can hire skates and take a spin at
Hôtel de Ville, Montparnasse and the Bassin de la Villette (the
canal basin by the Stalingrad metro station).

INTRODUCTION

The big boys of corporate accommodation are still on the prowl
with the idea of snatching up the most delectable morsels and
turning them into tasteless clones of their other chain products.
But new trends are emerging, partly stimulated by the general
economic slowdown. Some big boys have found that their
'palace hotel' expertise is cannot adapted to managing small
hotels and are selling. Others are offering franchises: a financial
guarantee and central buying to shore up independent but cash-
strapped owners. Thirdly, a few small family business partnerships
are creating an intriguing hybrid by buying and renovating little
old places and becoming 'chains' of smart designer hotels
that look and feel like real family-run, individually-designed
places... except that the managers change every few years
as their careers move them through the company's various
positions.

Lastly, more good little hotels are joining what the French call
'voluntary marketing chains' — clubs for like minded people —
in order to pool marketing resources and thus preserve their
independence and protect themselves from the raiders. They are
to be encouraged and we are delighted to have some of them
in this collection of small, independent hotels. Certain families
own three or four and run them in close collaboration with
their managers; one or two hotels are franchised, i.e. they use
a group's marketing capacity but are fully autonomous owners.

A younger generation is arriving, bringing a general upward
movement in 'services and equipment' and, of course, prices:
a two-star that refurbishes will generally aim to join the three-
star league and bang goes another of the cheaper, decent and
eminently friendly places we have known and loved for years.
But there are a few new ones coming in and I hope you will
find enough such places here if that's what you're looking for.

INTRODUCTION

What to expect   We hope to have explained the individuality and quirks of each
hotel so that you will only choose a place that suits you. The
range in these pages is broad, from our one and only *Pension de
Famille*, a French institution that is definitely only for those
who know and want exactly that kind of homely simplicity,
to two or three rather grand establishments where superior
comfort comes with genuine attentiveness – at four-star
prices. Obviously, the smaller the hotel, the more personal
the welcome. But do read our write-ups closely for details
and atmosphere.

Space   The greatest luxury in Paris is space. Even the more expensive
hotel rooms are generally small but there are exceptions – we
tell you about them all.

Noise   This dense, populous city is on a wonderfully human scale
but the traffic is dense too and streets can be noisy. In cheaper
hotels, noise can be due to thin walls and televisions – or late-
night revellers coming home. Double-glazing and air-
conditioning are becoming the norm in the more expensive
places but if you are a fresh air fiend and can't sleep with the
windows shut, bring earplugs. Or ask for a room *sur la cour*
(over the courtyard) – less view but less noise.

**How to use
this book**

Rooms & Bathrooms

Almost all hotels have a choice of single, double and twin rooms
and many places can turn two rooms into a self-contained suite,
so specify your needs when booking. A 'duplex' room is two
rooms above each other connected by a staircase but without a
kitchenette. All bedrooms have their own bath or shower room
with wc unless otherwise stated.

Disabled

All hotels with lifts will have rooms accessible to people of
limited mobility unless the lift only starts on the first floor or
stops at half-landings. Where relevant, such details are given in
italics at the bottom of the description. The few places that are
fully equipped to take wheelchair guests are listed in the Quick
Reference Index at the back of the book.

INTRODUCTION

Prices

The price range we give covers the lowest price for one person to the highest for two people. Differences may be due to seasons, room size, style or comfort, so the variations within those ranges can be considerable.

Taxe de séjour

Paris City Council levies a tax per person per night in Paris hotels. In 2002, it was 35cts for 1-star, 65cts for 2-star, 86cts for 3-star, €1 for 4-star. Some hotels include it in the price, some add it on - we can't specify which, so be prepared for a small extra sum per day on the bill.

Credit Cards

Only the Pension des Marronniers does not take credit cards. MasterCard and Visa are universally accepted; American Express sometimes; Diners Card hardly ever.

Breakfast

Unless we say otherwise, it will be basic continental: coffee, tea or chocolate with baguette, butter and jam plus a possible croissant and orange juice. 'Continental-plus' means this with, perhaps, cereals, yogurt and/or fruit. Buffet can be a help-yourself 'continental-plus' or a fabulous spread that virtually provides your daily intake of calories in one sitting. Breakfast in bed will almost always be continental. To make the most of every square centimetre, Paris hotel breakfast rooms are often in their stone-vaulted cellars. Magnificent examples of a well-tried building principle, they are, of course, 'authentic', 'original', 'fascinating', and can be rather stuffy.

Telephones

With few exceptions, all rooms have telephones; some can even supply a private line with your own number. Remember, however, to use hotel telephones only *in extremis* or if you are rich. The bills rarely fail to raise eyebrows, and temperatures.

All French phone numbers have ten digits, e.g. (0)5 05 25 35 45.

INTRODUCTION

You should know that:

- the zero (bracketed above) is for use when telephoning from inside France only, e.g. dial 05 15 25 35 45 from any private or public telephone;

- when dialling from outside France use the international access code, then the country code for France (33) then the last 9 digits of the number you want, e.g. 00 33 5 15 25 35 45;

- numbers beginning (0)6 are mobile phone numbers;

- to telephone from France
  - to Great Britain: 00 44 then the number without the first 0.
  - to North America: 00 1 then the number without the first 0.

Pillows and tea

If there is something you need and can't see, ask for it. The hotel may or may not be able to provide but you can only find out by asking. If you don't like the bolster, look in the cupboard for a pillow. If it's not there, ask. If you're particular about your tea, take your favourite tea-bags with you – French tea is often fairly standard.

Problems

If you have a problem, please first bring it up with the owner or manager: they are the obvious people to ask for immediate action. After all, you are paying to be looked after and if your hot water isn't hot or your bed isn't made by 5pm, well... it should be! Also, the manager's job is to keep you as happy as possible – he wants you to come back – but he can't solve a problem he doesn't know about. So do give them a chance to sort it out. However, if you try and don't succeed, or if you experience downright rudeness, then we need to know. Please write to us in such a case.

Parking

We tell you which hotels have their own car-parking arrangements but do not take these for granted: space must be booked at the same time as the room. The charge should be between € 15 and

INTRODUCTION

€30 per day (there are wild exceptions).

Tipping

By law, bills for hotels, cafés and restaurants in France must include the service charge, so one only tips for exceptional kindness or service.

Our title page pictures Each neighbourhood is introduced by an original pen and ink drawing by Aymeric Chastenet, a young Parisian cartoonist. He chose a few evocative street names and built a series of little scenes to illustrate them. We give the relevant street names and a brief English translation and hope they will amuse you and lead you to look even more closely at the infinite detail of Paris.

Environment We try to reduce our impact on the environment by:

• planting trees. We are officially Carbon Neutral®. The emissions directly related to paper production, printing and distribution of this book have been 'neutralised' through the planting of indigenous woodlands with Future Forests.

• re-using paper, recycling stationery, tins, bottles, etc.

• encouraging staff use of bicycles (they're loaned free) and encouraging car sharing.

• celebrating the use of organic, home – and locally-produced food.

• publishing books that support, in however small a way, the rural economy and small-scale businesses.

• running an Environmental Benefit Trust to stimulate business interest in the environment.•

We publish The Little Earth Book (www.littleearth.co.uk), a collection of essays on environmental issues. We also have a new title in production called The Little Food Book, another hard-hitting analysis – this time of the food industry.

INTRODUCTION

Subscriptions Owners pay to appear in this guide; their fee goes towards the costs of a sophisticated inspection system and the production of an all-colour book. We only include places and owners that we find positively special. There is a long waiting list of candidates and it is not possible for anyone to buy their way in.

Internet Our web site has online entries for all the places featured here and in our other books, with up-to-date information and direct links to their own email addresses and web sites. You'll find more about the site at the back of this book.

Disclaimer We make no claims to pure objectivity in choosing our Special Places to Stay. They are here because we like them. Our opinions and tastes are ours alone and this book is a statement of them; we hope that you will share them.

Finally Do let us know how you got on in these hotels — we value your feedback and recommendations enormously. Use the report form at the back of the book or email parishotels@sawdays.co.uk.

Ann Cooke-Yarborough

Plan of Paris Metro System

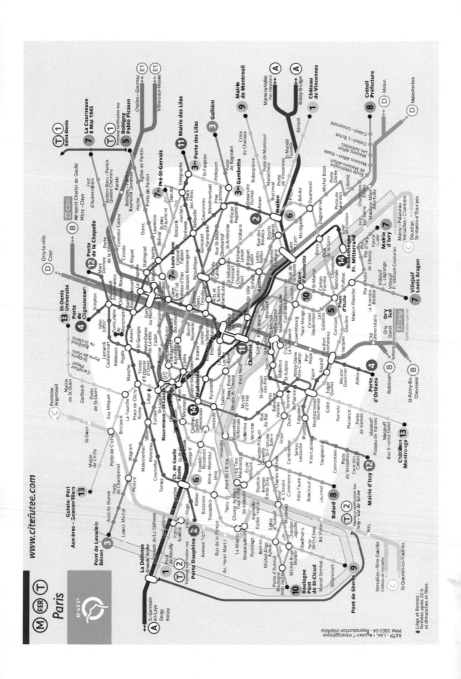

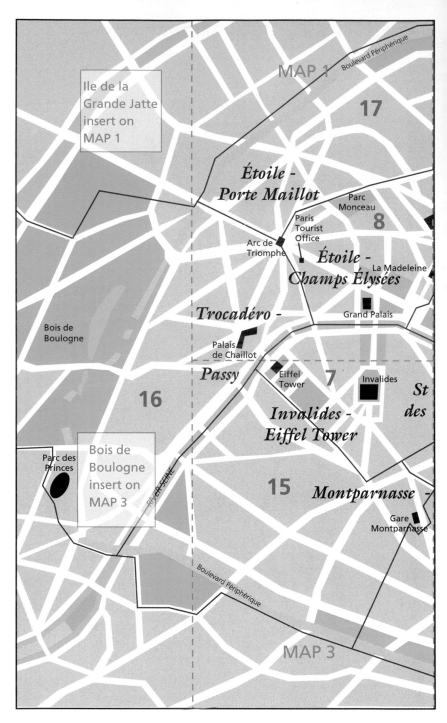

General Map with Arrondissements

Detailed maps are shown on the following pages.

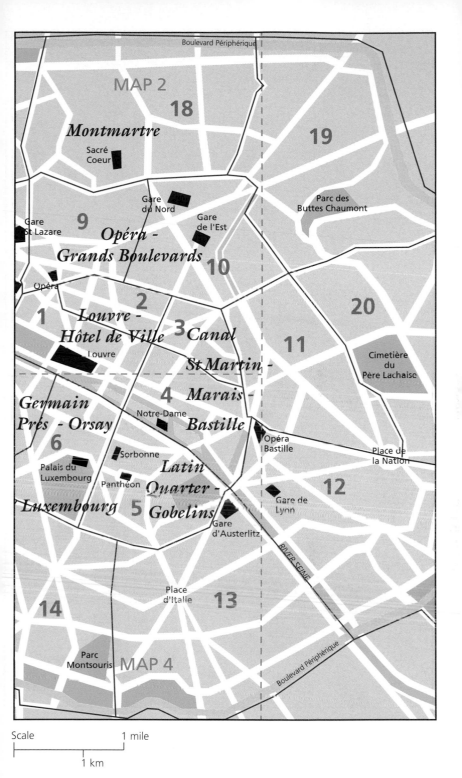

Scale

1 mile

1 km

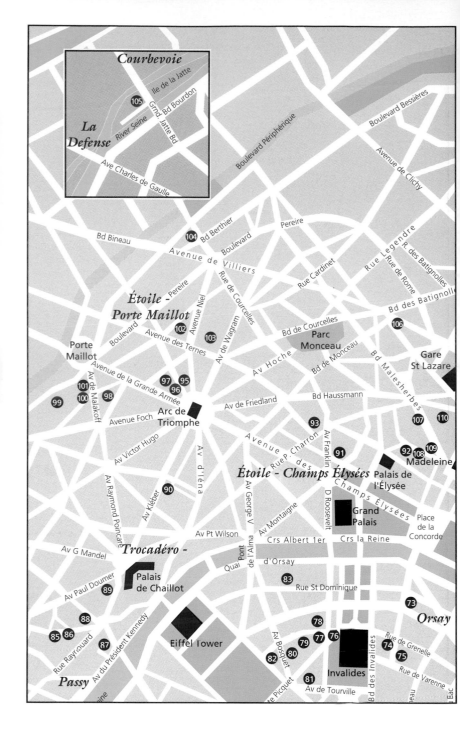

Map 1

Scale

1 mile

1 km

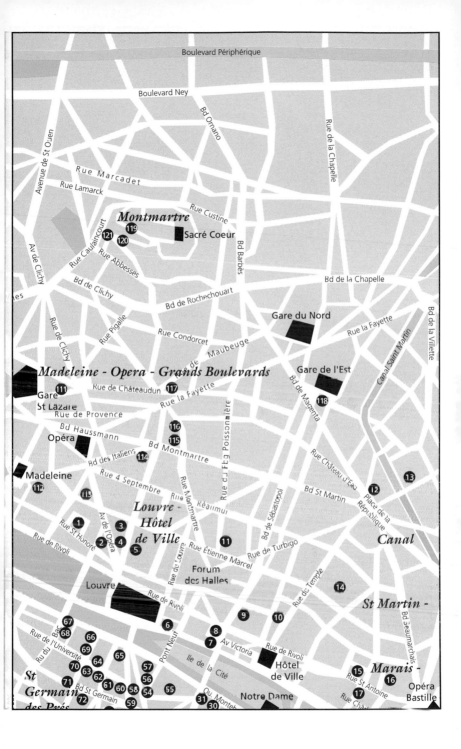

Map 2

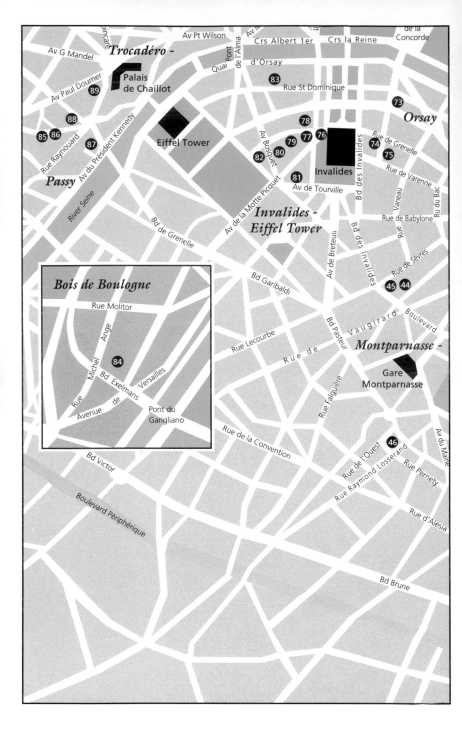

Map 3

Scale

1 mile

1 km

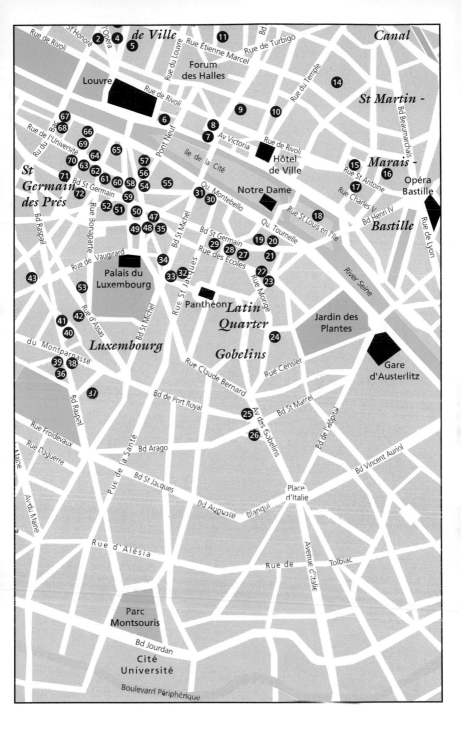

Map 4

LOUVRE - PALAIS ROYAL - HÔTEL DE VILLE

Rue du Pélican
Rue de l'Arbre Sec
Rue au Lard*
Rue des Bons Enfants

Pelican - Withered Tree - Bacon (formerly) - Good Children*

Hôtel des Tuileries

10 rue Saint Hyacinthe, 75001 Paris

The delicate listed façade of this quiet old *Relais du Silence* moves skywards to the rhythm of balconies, arches and mouldings. Inside, the charming Tuileries feels rather like a family house – the owners have been here for several generations. Great doors give onto a white hall with rugs, mirrors, pictures old and new, leading to the elegant little *salons*. A pretty lightwell illuminates this space and the basement breakfast room, a generous curving staircase leads upwards. Turkey rugs are everywhere but the oriental element is never excessive: one room is like a soft Persian tent, another has a clever yellow drapery over a white bed, there are Chinese-vase table lamps, paisley fabrics. Colours are skilfull – a white room with dark blue carpet, pale blue damask curtains and bedcover, a richly-coloured rug behind the delightful cane bedhead. Lighting is good, there are pretty antiques, country pieces, modern units, good marble bathrooms. The smaller rooms can feel cramped and higher prices are for the excellent deluxe rooms. *Modem connections in some rooms. Family apartments possible. Pets € 10. English, German, Italian and Spanish spoken.*

rooms	26: 10 doubles, 14 twins, 2 triples.
price	€ 136–€ 229. Children under 10 free.
meals	Buffet breakfast € 11.50; lunch & dinner on request.
metro	Tuileries (1), Pyramides (7).
RER	Auber.
buses	21 27 29 68 72 95
car park	Marché St Honoré.

Jean–Jacques Vidal

tel	(0)1 42 61 04 17
fax	(0)1 49 27 91 56
e-mail	hotel-des-tuileries@wanadoo.fr
web	www.hotel-des-tuileries.com

St Hyacinth was made a Dominican by St Dominic himself, eight centuries ago. He then dashed all over Eastern Europe, converting the tribes and earning the title of the Apostle of the North.

map 2   entry 1

Hôtel Londres-Saint Honoré
13 rue Saint Roch, 75001 Paris

There is something really appealing about the Berthouds' labyrinthine hotel in the middle of the Louvre-Opera-Concorde triangle. Lots of red gives it a rich feel, as does Madame's warm voice that welcomes you: this is a new career for her and she is thoroughly enjoying it. If you ask what that intriguing antique was designed for, she doesn't know either but is delighted to share the joke. Quantities of timbers speak of great age and venerability; she once found an American guest climbing the lovely staircase on all fours, reverently stroking each timber. Rooms are all shapes and sizes, mostly larger than the two-star average, and the red, white and blue colour scheme is used to great effect. It is uncluttered, unfrilled and extremely pleasant with decent tiled bathrooms and pretty lights. Hung with an artist friend's paintings, the first-floor sitting and breakfast rooms are also easy and light. Their other hotel, the plainer St Roch just up the road, a kind of 22-room 'annexe', is being done in the same style. *Internet access. Lift from first-floor reception level. five rooms have air conditioning. Pets €12. English spoken.*

The tiny antique shop clinging to the church opposite may indeed have been founded in 1638 but until recently it also said Coiffeur de Napoléon. He was a small man.

rooms	30: 17 doubles/twins, 12 singles, 1 suite for 5-6.
price	€64–€100, suite €200.
meals	Breakfast €6.50.
metro	Tuileries (1), Pyramides (7, 14).
RER	Châtelet-Les Halles.
buses	21 27 29 68 95
car park	Pyramides.

Monsieur & Madame Berthoud

tel	(0)1 42 60 15 62
fax	(0)1 42 60 16 00
e-mail	hotel.londres.st.honore@gofornet.com

Hôtel Thérèse

5 & 7 rue Thérèse, 75001 Paris

The newly-revived Thérèse is luscious: smart yet relaxedly informal, contemporary yet classic, rich dark colours with a few bright surprises making for warm, intelligent comfort. According to your mood, you can gather on the soft brown sofas of the aniseed-green front *salon* or sneak past the mushroom-hued desk into the dark-panelled library/bar space, just you, a book and peace. No French frillies here, but clean lines, excellent quality materials, lovely natural fabrics and delightful touches of exoticism: an African animal here, a Chinese porcelain stool there. Bedrooms, some large, some definitely small, have the same calm luxury; an original picture each; a variety of utterly pleasing colours, some lively, some muted (mauve/yellow, leaf green, beige/blue…); specially-made dark wooden furniture; superb bedding, of course, and perfect white-grey tiled bathrooms with wonderful old-style tap fittings beside all the right mod cons. A super vaulted breakfast room and friendly, intelligent young staff complete the picture of Sylvie de Lattre's new and very welcoming address bang in the centre of Paris. *English, German, Italian, Spanish spoken.*

rooms	43: 23 doubles, 17 twins, 3 junior suites for 4.
price	€125–€190, suite €250.
meals	Breakfast €12; lunch & dinner on request €15–€30.
metro	Pyramides (7, 14), Palais Royal (1).
RER	Auber.
buses	21 27 39 48 81 95
car park	Pyramides.

When Queen Marie-Thérèse died suddenly in 1683, her notoriously unfaithful husband Louis XIV declared majestically, "This is the only time she has ever pained me".

Sylvie de Lattre & Karine Sanchez

tel	(0)1 42 96 10 01
fax	(0)1 42 96 15 22
e-mail	hoteltherese@wanadoo.fr
web	www.hoteltherese.com

map 2   entry 3

Hôtel Molière
21 rue Molière, 75001 Paris

This is an enchantingly French hotel with a sensitive mixture of urban and country comforts. The big yellow lobby/*salon* is smart and rather grand with its *faux-marbre* columns and black and white upholstery but the welcome from the desk is gentle and warm – the new young owners infuse the place with their intelligent enthusiasm. Breakfast is a delight, its tempting buffet spread on a gingham cloth and bunched curtains giving a glimpse of the little cobbled green courtyard. There's also a small, deep-chaired *salon* round the corner for your quiet moments. Bedrooms are just as pretty with judicious use of nostalgic Jouy prints on walls and coordinated checks on quilts – or vice versa, or stripes, or sprigs... The Jouy colours go perfectly with the occasional antique: red and yellow, grey and green, blue and ivory, a little old writing desk, an unusual chair. Bathrooms, some vast, some very snug, may be modern and delicious or bask in the old-fashioned personality of built-in fittings and mosaic tiles. Interesing paintings, plants and ornaments give the Molière a well-cared-for feel. You will like it here. *English and Spanish spoken.*

Was the great comic dramatist Molière France's first celebrity? The son of a humble upholsterer, he rose so high that King Louis XIV was godfather to his first child.

rooms	33: 15 doubles, 10 twins/triples, 5 singles, 3 suites.
price	€125-€170, suites €275.
meals	Continental-plus breakfast €12.
metro	Palais Royal-Musée du Louvre (1, 7); Pyramides (7).
RER	Opéra-Auber.
buses	21 24 27 29 39 48 72 81 95
car park	Pyramides.

Patricia & Rémy Perraud

tel	(0)1 42 96 22 01
fax	(0)1 42 60 48 68
e-mail	info@hotel-moliere.fr
web	www.hotel-moliere.fr

Hôtel Washington Opéra
50 rue de Richelieu, 75001 Paris

Notice the quietly decorated Louis XV façade with its lovely painted frontage in this rather severe Parisian street: built in 1620 for Madame de Pompadour, it received the feminine touch. Then enter the luxury of soft silence in what is now the Washington Opéra, a smart, civilised, efficient little 'boutique' hotel. Typically French, the Louis XVI *salon* spreads its pale yellow elegance and dainty mural round the old marble fireplace. Up on the roof, overlooking the Palais Royal gardens, is a wonderful terrace for breakfast, tea and cocktails in summer. Otherwise, these delights take place in the well-laid-out semi-basement with its stocky armchairs and unusual brass-trimmed tables. The richly red or blue bedrooms are most stylish with clean-limbed elegant Gustavian furniture (a Swedish interpretation of the French Directoire style), some lovely wide Regency stripes or checks or discreet florals and excellent marble bathrooms. Rooms at the back give onto the old Palais Royal theatre, which has a fascinating back view, and occupants are serenaded by all the birds that dance in those trees. *Dutch, English, German, Italian and Spanish spoken.*

rooms	36: 16 doubles, 10 twins, 10 junior suites.
price	€ 215–€ 275, suites € 335.
meals	Buffet breakfast € 13, various meals on request.
metro	Palais Royal–Musée du Louvre (1, 7).
RER	Auber.
buses	29 39 48 81
car park	Rue Croix des Petits Champs.

Hacène Boudaa	
tel	(0)1 42 96 68 06
fax	(0)1 40 15 01 12
e-mail	hotel@washingtonopera.com
web	www.hotelwashingtonopera.com

The immense statesman Cardinal Richelieu left two famous deathbed statements: "My only enemies have been enemies of the State" and "Knowing how to dissemble is knowledge for kings".

map 2   entry 5

Le Relais du Louvre

19 rue des Prêtres St Germain l'Auxerrois, 75001 Paris

Look down the throats of gargoyles. Soak up the history. The Revolutionaries printed their newsletter in the cellar; the place inspired Puccini's Café Momus in *Bohême* and is utterly delightful, as are the charming young managers who greet you from the antique desk. Everywhere, antiques and oriental rugs complement the modernity of firm beds and perfect bathrooms. Front rooms look onto the church's Gothic flights of fancy and along to the austerely neo-classical Louvre; others give onto a light-filled patio. Top-floor junior suites have twin beds and a non-convertible sofa (no cluttering up), pastel walls, exuberant upholstery and heaps of light from mansard windows. The apartment (pictured) is big and beautiful with fireplace, books, music, old engravings and a superb veranda kitchen. Other, smaller rooms are luminous, fresh and restful – yellow, a favourite colour, brings sunny moods into small spaces. You feel softly secluded and coddled everywhere. The sense of service is highly developed and as there is no breakfast room, breakfast comes to you. On each floor, two rooms can make a family suite. *English, German, Italian, Spanish spoken.*

The best view over Paris is just beside you – and it's free! Take the lift to the terrace roof of the Samaritaine store and admire the city from its very centre.

rooms	21: 4 doubles; 14 doubles/twins; 2 junior suites; 1 apartment for 4.
price	€99–€180; suites €205–€244; apartment €380.
meals	Breakfast (in bedroom) €10; lunch & dinner on request €10–€30.
metro	Louvre-Rivoli (1), Pont Neuf (7).
RER	Châtelet-Les Halles.
buses	67 69 72 74 85
car park	Consult hotel.

Sophie Aulnette

tel	(0)1 40 41 96 42
fax	(0)1 40 41 96 44
e-mail	contact@relaisdulouvre.com
web	www.relaisdulouvre.com

Grand Hôtel de Champagne

17 rue Jean Lantier, 75001 Paris

Built in 1562 (spot the date on the wooden pillar by reception) on a street corner that was first recorded in the 13th century, the Champagne has been a monastery, a school and an inn: rooms were never big, corridors twist and turn and the vast expanse of the timbered, panelled ground floor does not prepare you for the medieval proportions upstairs – don't bring a whole wardrobe. The smart Louis XIII dining room is big too, in its crimson and gold regalia. This is where you can indulge in a remarkably full and varied breakfast buffet. Bedrooms are sweetly, cosily cottagey, with more timbers and beams, cords and canopy effects, spriggy or stripey wallpapers, the odd little antique and glances at the great periods of French style – Louis XIII, XV and XVI. There are nooks, corners and crannies, as dictated by the ancient layout, and the deluxe suites occupy two or three old rooms each. Bathrooms are imaginatively pretty. It is altogether enfolding and peaceful. Staff and manager are relaxed and smiling – he clearly likes his job and enjoys making clients as comfortable as possible. *Two floors are classified non-smoking. English and Italian spoken.*

rooms	43: 23 doubles, 14 twins, 3 triples, 3 junior suites.
price	€ 135–€ 195, suites € 220–€ 320.
meals	Full buffet breakfast € 12.30.
metro	Châtelet (1, 4, 7, 11, 14), Pont Neuf (7).
RER	Châtelet-Les Halles.
buses	21 38 58 67 69 74 76 81 85
car park	Belle Jardinière.

Madame Lauferon, Monsieur Herbron

tel	(0)1 42 36 60 00
fax	(0)1 45 08 43 33
e-mail	champaigne@hotelchampaigne.com
web	hotelchampaigneparis.com

For two centuries (16th-18th), the whole neighbourhood was occupied by master craftsmen and their brotherhoods: 'goldsmiths, silversmiths, tailors, cobblers was here'.

map 2   entry 7

Hôtel Britannique

20 avenue Victoria, 75001 Paris

Originally run by the British Baxters, the *Britannique* is now owned by an ex-naval man with a passion for Turner – the great painter's *Jessica* greets you in the lobby, copies of his oils and water colours adorn the corridors, the *Fighting Temeraire* dominates the deeply comfortable *salon* alongside a model galleon, an HMV gramophone horn and some fine books. Do take the staircase: elegantly pink and grey, it has handsome old fitted oak chests on each landing. The average-to-small rooms are all decorated with the same custom-made elements, pastel walls, heavy green-leaf/red-grape fabrics, boxes of pot-pourri for extra florality and very adequate bathrooms. Nice modern double-framed mirrors too. The higher floors have views over roofs and treetops. Plants, furniture, parasols and urns are sold on the pavement below – it's lively and fun in the daytime, quietish at night. In the semi-basement, the breakfast room is now prettily blue and yellow with a long marble buffet table in a rustic alcove. It is simply comfortable with no ancient flourishes and a generally friendly reception from staff in stripey waistcoats. *English and German spoken.*

During the 1st World War, the hotel was offered to American and English Quaker volunteers tending civilian victims - a service rendered by the Quakers in wars all over the world.

rooms	39: 23 doubles, 9 twins, 6 singles, 1 junior suite for 4.
price	€130–€180; suite €280.
meals	Buffet breakfast €12.
metro	Châtelet (1, 4, 7, 11).
RER	Châtelet-Les Halles.
buses	21 38 58 67 69 74 76 81 85
car park	Hôtel de Ville.

J-F Danjou

tel	(0)1 42 33 74 59
fax	(0)1 42 33 82 65
e-mail	mailbox@hotel-britannique.fr
web	www.hotel-britannique.fr

Hôtel Saint Merry

78 rue de la Verrerie, 75004 Paris

If you love the old and utterly unusual and are not afraid of a few stairs, this is for you. The hotel huddles against the late-Gothic church of St Merry whose clock tower cornice thrusts its way into the top-floor suite; in the first-floor reception you find an elaborate pew, linen-fold panels, a telephone in a confessional; in another room, a couple of buttresses provide the most original of low-flying bed canopies. From *brocante* and flea market came the wherewithal to make the old house worthy of its origins, neo-Gothic pieces were reworked to create this astounding environment, atmospheric paintings chosen to enhance it. The sober décor sets off the festival of carving: plain velvet or 'medieval-stripe' fabrics, great cast-iron light fittings, original beams and stonework – and some strangely colourful bathrooms (the new shower rooms are excellent). The big rooms are almost majestic, the cheaper ones are smaller and more basic, the suite a masterpiece of style and adaptation (surely Paris's only Gothic *salon*?) *Difficult motor access in pedestrian street and no lift in hotel (four floors). English, Japanese and Spanish spoken.*

rooms	12: 6 doubles, 3 twins, 2 triples, 1 suite for 4–5.
price	€146–€250; suite €305–€370.
meals	Breakfast (in bedroom) €10.
metro	Hôtel de Ville (1, 11), Châtelet (1, 4, 7, 11, 14).
RER	Châtelet-Les Halles.
buses	38 47 75
car park	St Martin.

The street has been called Verrerie (glassworks) since 1187! The painters on glass - enamellers, glass-blowers, rosary and necklace-makers - lived and worked here in their corporations for centuries.

Pierre Juin

tel	(0)1 42 78 14 15
fax	(0)1 40 29 06 82
e-mail	hotelstmerry@wanadoo.fr
web	www.hotelmarais.com

map 2   entry 9

Hôtel du Bourg Tibourg

19 rue du Bourg Tibourg, 75004 Paris

Is it Neo-Byzantine? Gothic? Moorish? All of those – plus Jacques Garcia's inventive flourishes. He and the Costes family, a proven designer/owner team, have conjured up this latest concoction in a careful delirium of detail: totally original furniture, halogen lamps disguised as medieval torches, a real Aubusson tapestry, a vast Arabian chandelier against kilometres of striped and crushed and brass-studded plush. Gothic red and black, Moroccan blue and gold, oriental green and the four-leafed clover are much used; it's all luscious and touchable. Every room is a variation on the jewel-box theme. They are generally not big but storage is adequate and one room has a brilliant walk-in cupboard space behind its great brown velvet nest of a bed, lit by two atmospherically red fringed lamps. Breakfast is in the 17th-century cellar among more purple plushness. In contrast to these reminders of bygone luxury, bathrooms are properly 21st century with excellent mirrors and all the bits. Staff are young and bright, too, delighted with their new surroundings and ever willing to help. *English, German, Italian, Polish, Russian and Spanish spoken.*

rooms	30: 16 doubles, 7 twins, 5 singles, 2 junior suites for 3.
price	€150-€250, suites €350.
meals	Breakfast €12; afternoon tea available.
metro	Hôtel de Ville (1, 11).
RER	Châtelet-Les Halles.
buses	38 47 67 69 75 96
car park	Place Baudroyer.

In the 13th century, this area, between Rue de La Verrerie and Rue Sainte Croix de la Bretonnerie, was recorded as a little hamlet way out in the country called Bourg Tibourd.

Madame Costes

tel	(0)1 42 78 47 39
fax	(0)1 40 29 07 00
e-mail	hotel.du.bourg.tibourg@wanadoo.fr
web	www.hoteldubourgtibourg.com

Hôtel Victoires Opéra

56 rue Montorgueil, 75002 Paris

From the lively pedestrian street where neat little shops beckon and cafés spill over the pavements – wonderfully Parisian – enter the Victoires and another universe. Calm and contemporary, small and perfectly formed, it has sober dark sofas against eggshell walls, clean austere lines in contrast to bright contrived flowers and artfully non aligned photographs. Bedrooms are unfrillily businesslike too. Materials are of high quality – fabulous satin silk curtains, soft wool bedcovers edged in wide finely-striped ribbon – and the decorative scheme is the same throughout. Each room has elegant brown or yellow stripes behind an impeccable two-wood bed panel and dark furniture, tall dark curtains, snow-white pillows. Bathrooms are cleanly beautiful in tile and marble, lamps are thin brass sticks, storage is perfect and the four-star extras are there. In sensual counterpoint to all these straight lines there are female portraits or nudes, including some Modigliani favourites. Then descend to the orange and red vaulted breakfast room for a delicious wake-up. Attentive service is one of the commitments of this smart new hotel. *Arabic and English spoken.*

rooms	28: 20 doubles, 4 twins, 4 suites.
price	€215–€275, suites €335.
meals	Buffet breakfast €12.
metro	Étienne Marcel (4).
RER	Châtelet-Les Halles.
buses	29 67 74 85
car park	Consult hotel.

Hakim Boudaa

tel	(0)1 42 36 41 08
fax	(0)1 45 08 08 79
e-mail	hotel@victoiresopera.com
web	www.hotelvictoiresopera.com

Whose victory? Place des Victoires first had a vast statue of battling King Louis XIV, then a revolutionary pyramid to freedom, then a naked Napoleonic general. In 1816 the Restoration restored... King Louis.

map 2   entry 11

CANAL ST MARTIN - MARAIS - BASTILLE

Passage des Singes
Rue du Pas de la Mule
Rue de la Tacherie
Rue des Mauvais Garçons

Monkeys - Mule's Step - Staining - Bad Boys

Hôtel Gilden Magenta
35 rue Yves Toudic, 75010 Paris

In a corner of genuine people's Paris that is attracting trendy cafés and interesting eateries, this modest, friendly hotel stands between the tranquil St Martin Canal and the mad dash of the Place de la République. It has always been a hotel, one of a row of harmonious, unpretentious 1890s buildings, with an old bakery on the corner. The big hall is due for radical refurbishment in 2003 – until then, it's a theatrical, kitschy legacy. The relaxed new owners are attentive to detail and should look after you well. Beyond the semi-veranda breakfast space, the restful green flowering patio is just the spot for summer mornings beneath the giant sun yellow parasols; bedrooms in the garden building give onto this patio. All rooms and bathrooms are gradually being renovated: clean, spring-like décor, pretty primrose-painted furniture, the odd pine-slatted wall and excellent little shower rooms. Character too: the quadruple has a bit of timber framing in the middle and from some front rooms you can see down to the barges and boats cruising along above road level. A super relaxed atmosphere and excellent value. *English, German and Spanish spoken.*

rooms	27: 12 doubles, 6 twins, 6 singles, 2 triples, 1 quadruple.
price	€ 56–€ 90.
meals	Buffet breakfast € 6.50.
metro	République (3, 5, 8, 9, 11), Jacques Bonsergent (5).
RER	Gare du Nord.
buses	54 56 75
car park	Boulevard Magenta (consult hotel).

Gilbert Pouleur

tel	(0)1 42 40 17 72
fax	(0)1 42 02 59 66
e-mail	hotel.gilden.magenta@multi-micro.com
web	www.multi-micro.com/hotel.gilden.magenta/

The Gilden's emblem is that atmospheric footbridge where Arletty, Jouvet & Co. hang out, smoke, kiss, fight... in Marcel Carné's iconic 1938 film Hôtel du Nord.

map 2   entry 12

Un Petit Palais

Brickhouse-sur-canal, 75010 Paris

An exceptional find! The little brick palace is your chance to watch life in the raw. Passing through the old lock, admire the nuts and bolts of the two bridges – swing-bridge below, footbridge above. On the canal, the bargeman lives the life of a nomad, his tiny living quarters squeezed like an afterthought onto the end of his long narrow cargo carrier. From the near-privacy of your fenced piece of garden beneath the spreading chestnut trees, you can observe at close quarters tons of coal, gravel and sand, those materials dragged filthy from the entrails of the earth that we no longer recognise in our pre-packaged age. They travel in heaps. On some heaps you may even see unfettered dogs and live chickens, throwbacks to the distant days of natural production and farmyard freedom. Inside your refuge you will be totally private – boarded windows allow for no peerings-in – to enjoy simplicity beyond belief: a solid wooden chair folds away to leave room for the bedroll, cleverly stored in the cupboard section where basic facilities are also hidden. The shoes are for you to wear for those smart evenings out (see below) – few owners care this much.

rooms	One unique space for all guests, all activities.
price	One tin of Church's superior black boot polish.
meals	Hook and line provided for canalside self-sufficiency.
metro	Brickhouse Roc.
car park	Barge holds available.

The old Parisian custom of midnight dried-leaf gathering is still practised on this stretch: the crumbled leaves are marinaded in canal water at dawn; the juice is a guaranteed cure for Goodoledays Syndrome.

Monsieur la Brique
tel (0)7 57 75 57
e-mail brickhouse@eaudecanal.fr

Hôtel de Saintonge

16 rue Saintonge, 75003 Paris

On the edge of the lively Marais district with its boutiques and bistros, its mansions and museums, this street is almost provincially quiet. Pierre Juin, the new owner who also owns the St Merry, is planning to refurbish the hotel whose good bones – beams and stones – can be seen beyond the modern garb of new flooring and high desk in the lobby and high vaulted breakfast cellar. Two ground-floor rooms that lead off the little patio, occupied in all weathers by a half-naked bather, are countrified and pretty-print-floral with high iron beds and stable doors. The topmost room is the big suite, up a flight of stairs to the rafters. Its double room has a superbly curvy Louis XVI bed and cane furniture, its bathroom is beige, its "children's room" a bit disappointing in its orange sofabed and minimal furniture. Most other rooms are beamed and a few have been very pleasingly renovated in a light, fresh style with brass beds, possibly a gauzy canopy, an arty inlaid table, lots of personality (pictured). Older rooms have decent colour schemes, cane furniture and beige bathrooms and await their turn. A quiet, reliable hotel in a really interesting area. *English spoken*

rooms	23. 17 doubles, 5 twins, 1 suite for 4.
price	€ 105–€ 115, suite € 170.
meals	Continental buffet breakfast € 10.
metro	Filles du Calvaire (8).
RER	Gare du Nord.
buses	20 29 65
car park	Rue de Bretagne.

No saints here: Saintonge was an early independent province of western France that was gathered to the crown of France by King Charles V in 1352. Its 'capital' is Saintes.

Pierre Juin

tel	(0)1 42 77 91 13
fax	(0)1 48 87 76 41
e-mail	hotelsaintonge@hotmail.fr
web	www.hotelmarais.com

map 2   entry 14

Hôtel Saint Paul Le Marais

8 rue de Sévigné, 75004 Paris

In among the old old buildings, the cafés, boutiques and mansions of the Marais, this hotel, built as a convent in the 17th century, still shows a few of its original beams and pillars but bedroom furniture is all new carved oak and bathrooms are being renovated in excellent fashion. The red and gold lobby with its smart brocade chairs, inviting little bar and bunched curtains is lit from the street and from a planted patio where tables can be set in summer. The stone breakfast vault in the cellar offers a generous and varied buffet that is worth getting up for. Bedrooms seem to be all shapes, sizes and quirks: a little child's sleeping platform with tiny washbasin in miniature cupboard, a muslin-canopied bed, a big bathroom with jacuzzi, another platform with a desk tucked right under a steeply sloping ceiling, a sunny little single like a pale blue nursery. It is quite old-fashioned, in keeping with the building, fairly floral, endearing and very friendly; each room is soundproofed and has a kettle kit. Madame Leguide and her new manager, ever willing to help and advise, create a comforting sense of welcome. *English spoken.*

Opposite, an imposing portal leads to Bouthillier de Chavigny's 17th-century mansion: high, gracious windows and a dozen red chargers in the courtyard - the only listed fire station for miles.

rooms	28: 12 doubles, 5 twins, 9 singles, 2 triples.
price	€ 115–€ 210.
meals	Buffet breakfast € 10.
metro	St Paul (4).
RER	Châtelet-Les Halles, Gare de Lyon.
buses	69 76 96
car park	Baudoyer.

Michèle Leguide & Riadh Soufi

tel	(0)1 48 04 97 27
fax	(0)1 48 87 37 04
e-mail	stpaulmarais@hotellerie.net
web	www.hotel-paris-marais

Hôtel de la Place des Vosges

12 rue de Birague, 75004 Paris

The five smallest rooms in this tiny hotel have been fabulously refurbished with lovely fabrics and deluxe marble bathrooms: small but perfectly formed. A modest neighbour of the oldest, loveliest square in Paris, it is still a friendly, unpretentious hotel where an air of relaxed hard work seems to have come down the centuries and the dynamic owner has time to chat with visitors beneath the old beams and advise on what to do; indeed, service and flexibility are their priorities. Expect less space above the ground floor. The tiny staircase (the lift goes from 1st to 4th floors; luggage carried by staff) and limited storage preclude large bags. Other rooms are being done up, bedding is new, the décor is still simple pink and beige with miniature but adequate shower and bathrooms. An ideal family hideaway, the top floor has a view of the Bastille column from its attic windows. If you travel light, this is a wonderful part of Paris to be in, rich in history and alive with 21st-century Parisians active in fashion and the arts. English spoken. *Various room arrangements possible: ask when booking. Cancellation policy is 72 hours notice in writing.*

rooms	16: 10 doubles, 5 twins, 1 family room.
price	€ 101–€ 140.
meals	Breakfast € 6.
metro	Bastille (1, 5, 8), St Paul (1), Sully Morland (7).
RER	Châtelet-Les Halles, Gare de Lyon.
buses	20 29 69 76 86 87 96
car park	16 rue St Antoine.

That vast beam was 800 years old when it was felled in the 1600s to build this 4-storey mule master's house. From ground-floor up: stable, hay loft, master's quarters, stable boys' garrets.

Renata Sibiga

tel	(0)1 42 72 60 46
fax	(0)1 42 72 02 64
e-mail	hotel.place.des.vosges@gofornet.com

map 4   entry 16

Hôtel du 7è Art
20 rue Saint Paul, 75004 Paris

The ultimate in film fame: Harry Potter was here in 2001... The old black and white image of film is lovingly tended here, as light-hearted and eternally youthful as the stars of yesteryear. Besides a delightful little hotel, there is a lively bar where log fires burn in winter and you can even buy mementos of the great names. The charming young owners and staff have thought of everything, including a laundry room and a trio of fitness machines to maintain your Hollywood muscles in decadent Paris. Black and white are the theme throughout – viz. that checked floor in the dining room – and a multitude of old film posters decorate the walls. Up the black-carpeted stairs, the bedrooms are softly, unaggressively decorated – some hessian walls, some pine slatting, brown carpets and multi-pastel piqué bedcovers – and have white and black bathrooms with the occasional star-studded shower curtain. Some rooms are pretty small, some have modem sockets or ceiling fans, the atmosphere is peaceful (the bar closes at midnight) and the oldest residential part of Paris is all around you. Simply a very special place. *English, German and Spanish spoken.*

rooms	23: 15 doubles, 7 twins, 1 single.
price	€58-€120.
meals	Continental-plus breakfast €7; bar snacks €8-€10.
metro	St Paul (1), Pont Marie (7).
RER	Châtelet-Les Halles.
buses	69 96
car park	Pont Marie.

Just over the road, do visit the Village St Paul, a series of old, twisty courtyards full of antique shops and art galleries; and beyond, remains of the 12th-century city ramparts.

Michel et Yolène

tel	(0)1 44 54 85 00
fax	(0)1 42 77 69 10
e-mail	hotel7art@wanadoo.fr

Hôtel du Jeu de Paume
54 rue Saint Louis en l'Île, 75004 Paris

Above: three storeys soar to the roof timbers of a 17th-century 'tennis' court – astounding. Below: genuine care from mother and daughter, fresh flowers, time for everyone, super staff. It's exceptional. Provençal in style, unique in atmosphere, smallish rooms give onto quiet courtyard gardens, have rich fabrics, pale walls, good bathrooms, old beams, stones, parquet. Duplexes have tiny staircases and cupboards below; some rooms show the building's beautiful beamy skeleton, some have little terraces; the secluded new apartments over the street have superb tall windows, space and style. We love it hugely – for its sense of history, eccentricities, aesthetic ironies, peaceful humour and feel of home; and for its unconventional attitudes and relaxed yet thoroughly efficient staff – so what matter that storage is limited? The lounge has *objets*, art, deep leather sofas round a carved fireplace and Scoop the soft gold dog; breakfast is beneath the magnificent timbers by the surrealistic columns; work-out is in vaulted cellars (billiards, bikes, sauna). "Quite exceptionally polite, friendly staff": a reader. *English, German, Russian, Spanish spoken.*

rooms	29 + 2 apartments: 25 double/twins, 1 triple, 2 duplex, 2 suites; 2 apartments.
price	€152–€275, suites €450, apartments €470–€520.
meals	Breakfast €14; lunch & dinner on request €15–€50.
metro	Pont Marie (7), Cité (1), St Paul (1).
RER	St Michel-Notre Dame.
buses	67
car park	Pont Marie.

Elyane Prache & Nathalie Heckel

tel	(0)1 43 26 14 18
fax	(0)1 40 46 02 76
web	www.jeudepaumehotel.com

The jeu de paume, the Italian ancestor of tennis, was all the rage in the 1600s. King Louis XIII allowed developers onto the island on condition that a palm game court was built. Plus ça change...

map 4   entry 18

LATIN QUARTER - GOBELINS

Rue du Petit Moine
Rue de l'Arbalète
Rue du Chat qui Pêche
Rue des Anglais

Little Monk - Crossbow - Fishing Cat - The English

Hôtel de Notre Dame

19 rue Maître Albert, 75005 Paris

Hidden from the tourist tides in a select little area, yet a stone's throw from Notre Dame, the fine old frontage opens onto a superb tapestry, bits of antiquity on oriental rugs and deep armchairs. Open is the word: these people genuinely like people and greet you with smiles and humour. As does the brilliant new conservatory-like breakfast room: big window to the street, 'rusted' tables, metal chairs with soft yellow cushions. If the convoluted corridors declare the age of the building (1600s), contemporary style dictates their smart look. Bedrooms also mix old and new. There are beams and exposed stones – some enormous – and cathedral views through smaller windows on higher floors. Fittings and furniture are in custom-made pale curvy wood, spotlights are discreet, new padded upholstery is warm and colourful with modern mixes of yellow, red and blue and the translucent screen doors to bathrooms are an excellent idea for small layouts (not all baths are full size). The black eunuch officially portrayed as Marie-Antoinette's feathered fan bearer lived here... A particularly welcoming place. *English and German spoken*

rooms	34: 26 doubles, 8 twins.
price	€ 139–€ 150.
meals	Breakfast € 7.
metro	Maubert Mutualité (10).
RER	St Michel-Notre Dame.
buses	47 63 86 87
car park	La Grange.

Monsieur Fouhety

tel	(0)1 43 26 79 00
fax	(0)1 46 33 50 11
e-mail	hotel.denotredame@libertysurf.fr
web	www.notre-dame-hotel.com

Master Albert (Magister Albertus, contracted to Maubert) was a preacher, teacher, philosopher and alchemist of persuasive power. He also built a walking talking automaton - in 1254!

map 4   entry 19

Hôtel Abbatial Saint Germain

46 boulevard St Germain, 75005 Paris

Relaxed and affable, Michel Sahuc is an enthusiast and his style informs his hotel: the receptionist may choose the music playing over the desk but the gently smart-stripey *salon* with its soft orange armchairs, long leather sofa and great gilt-framed mirror is always quiet; the Italianate landscape mural in the vaulted breakfast room – yes, a basement with sky – has distant cousins in all bedrooms: plaster relief pictures of Venuses and cherubs, arabesques and sibyls. Rooms are mostly a decent size and almost all have two windows. Different-coloured walls, varying from pastels to stronger, are another unusual feature here but furniture is classically pretty caned Louis XVI style or more severe dark polished wood, with good prints for curtains and quilted bedcovers and perfectly adequate bathrooms. A few rooms at the top, including one little single, have fabulous views swinging round from the colonnade of the Pantheon on its hill across the roofscape to the north rose of Notre Dame on her island, all within a few minutes' walk. A friendly, unpretentious place. *Internet access. English, Portuguese and Spanish spoken.*

rooms	43: 22 doubles, 14 twins, 7 singles.
price	€ 100–€ 150.
meals	Continental buffet breakfast € 8.
metro	Maubert Mutualité (10).
RER	St Michel-Notre Dame.
buses	47 63 86 87
car park	St Germain.

The abbey in question is over the road: St Nicolas de Chardonnet has become the hub of the traditionalist Catholic movement and the deep bells bring in the crowds from far and wide.

Michel Sahuc

tel	(0)1 46 34 02 12
fax	(0)1 43 25 47 73
e-mail	abbatial@club-internet.fr
web	www.abbatial.com

Hôtel Agora Saint Germain
42 rue des Bernardins, 75005 Paris

Deep in the heart of the Latin Quarter, one of the oldest centres of learning in Europe, here is a quiet place to stay just a stone's throw from the fashionable animation of St Germain, the student buzz of St Michel and the rafts of history that carry Notre Dame on her island. The generous, well-lit hall, the pretty glassed-in patio and the comfortable armchairs are greeting enough – then you'll be welcomed by the charming receptionist, or Madame Sahuc herself, youthful and bright. There is an atmosphere of relaxed, feminine attention to detail here. Even if some of the rooms are looking rather dated in their beiges, Madame has plans for the years to come and redecoration has brought more fashionable blue, yellow and white, or salmon-pink and orange, to others. There are good fabrics, a few fringed lampshades, lots of mirrors, some round, some oval, and all rooms are hung with amusing 1920s fashion prints and furnished with good solid French furniture. The old-stone basement breakfast room feels airy with its ginger mats, tapestry chairs and monogrammed china. A good reliable address. English, German and Spanish spoken.

rooms	39. 22 doubles, 9 twins, 7 singles, 1 triple.
price	€ 109–€ 159.
meals	Continental buffet breakfast € 8.
metro	Maubert Mutualité (10).
RER	St Michel-Notre Dame.
buses	47 63 86 87
car park	St Germain.

Pascale Sahuc

tel	(0)1 46 34 13 00
fax	(0)1 46 34 75 05
e-mail	agorastg@club-internet.fr
web	www.agorasaintgermain.com

The college for priests founded nearby in 1244 by the intriguingly named Étienne de Lexington of the Bernardine Order only lasted for about a hundred years - but the order lives still on the street corners.

map 4   entry 21

Hôtel Minerve

13 rue des Écoles, 75005 Paris

The Minerve, Eric Gaucheron's second hotel (his family also own the Familia next door), has his eagerly attentive, friendly touch – as well as the stimulating university life outside. The red-carpeted corridors lead to rooms that are mostly not huge but often use the classic, cunning bed alcove for storage space (all beds are new). The higher you are the longer the view (Notre Dame and the Seine, on the street side of course) and top-floor rooms have some wild and wonderful timbers over their quirky shapes and some rich red, gold and ivory colour schemes. Walls are gradually being decorated with those excellent sepia murals of French monuments, all different. Décor varies from brightly contemporary to soothingly granny, there are damask and satin, timber and tile, some nice old bits of furniture and gilt-framed mirrors, some recent built-in cupboards, decent bathrooms of varying sizes (the new ones are splendid). The lobby/*salon* is generously big, light and airy with pleasant repro furniture, tapestries and bookcases and the breakast room's original wall and ceiling paintings are a delight. Superb meeting room too. *English spoken.*

Seats of learning galore. In Rue Cardinal Lemoine, that cleric founded the Collège Cardinal Lemoine in 1305; in 1332, a priest from Arras started a school for poor children in Rue d'Arras.

rooms	54: 44 doubles/twins, 7 singles, 3 family rooms for 3-4.
price	€79–€160.
meals	Breakfast €7.
metro	Jussieu (7, 10), Maubert Mutualité (10).
RER	Cluny-La Sorbonne.
buses	47 63 67 86 87
car park	Lagrange.

Éric Gaucheron & Sylvie Roger

tel	(0)1 43 26 26 04
fax	(0)1 44 07 01 96
e-mail	minerve@hotellerie.net
web	www.hotel-paris-minerve.com

Familia Hôtel

11 rue des Écoles, 75005 Paris

It is well named! and glows under the care and attention showered by Éric, his wife Sylvie, their little Charles and his wonderfully energetic parents. It has a grand-looking balconied face but the family earnestly want to welcome you just as friends. Beyond the hall, hand-painted by an artist friend, is the newly-renovated rich red breakfast *salon* (cornices, mouldings, *trompe-lœil*...) where the Gaucherons' collection of leather-bound tomes and the thick Turkey rug give a homely feel. Bedrooms are warmly unpretentious. They are not large or 'Parisian chic' but each has either a lovely Paris fresco, a wall of ancient stones, an old carved bedhead or a balcony onto the fascinating street life – the ground-floor room even has a grand canopied bed. Carpets, wallpapers, bedcovers and curtains, not brilliantly trendy or stunningly matched, are somehow comfortingly provincial. Renovations are constant and it's all spotless. Front rooms look across the wide street to a rich jumble of old buildings with the Île Saint Louis just beyond. Ask Éric anything – he will answer willingly, at length and in fast English. *English and Spanish spoken.*

rooms	30: 23 doubles/twins, 6 singles, 1 quadruple.
price	€ 70-€ 170.
meals	Breakfast € 6.
metro	Jussieu (7, 10), Maubert Mutualité (10).
RER	Cluny-La Sorbonne.
buses	47 63 67 86 87
car park	Lagrange.

Éric Gaucheron

tel	(0)1 43 54 55 27
fax	(0)1 43 29 61 77
e-mail	familia.hotel@libertysurf.fr
web	www.hotel-paris-familia.com

This is a typical Style Noble C19 Haussmann building, i.e. it has balconies on 2nd, 3rd and 5th floors. Non-nobles lack that 3rd-floor superior touch. Look around you for examples.

map 4   entry 23

Hôtel Résidence Saint Christophe
17 rue Lacépède, 75005 Paris

The Saint Christophe is quiet and reassuring, its owners attentive and human. They have taken up their new profession with serious energy and gusto. In the old Latin Quarter underneath the Montagne Sainte Geneviève, the hotel has a long history of serving the community in various guises. The big attractive sitting room has light flooding in through a wall of window onto a magnificently carved antique *armoire*. Upstairs, although the décor is the same in every bedroom, the Robat brothers are making sure that quality reigns. Walls have a pinky-yellow sponged wallpaper, bedcovers are quilted in red satiny stuff, bedheads and furniture, including the genuine Vth-Republic minibars, is Louis XV or Louis XVI, bathrooms are decent in beige marble (some have windows to the outside that are disguised as mirrors – very surprising), and the overall atmosphere is of good bourgeois comfort. In the morning, breakfast is served in the white-walled, mirrored basement where upholstered Louis XV chairs and a *trompe-l'œil* mural of Paris put you in the picture for the day. *Internet access. English and Portuguese spoken.*

rooms	31: 15 doubles, 10 twins, 6 singles.
price	€ 104–€ 125.
meals	Continental-plus breakfast € 8.
metro	Monge (7).
RER	Gare d'Austerlitz, Luxembourg.
buses	47 89
car park	Patriarches.

On its 'mountain', the Pantheon was first dedicated to Geneviève. Legend says that she saved Paris from Attila the Hun in AD 451 by spitting on him. She became the city's patron saint when she died at 92.

Daniel & Jean Robat

tel	(0)1 43 31 81 54
fax	(0)1 43 31 12 54
e-mail	saintchristophe@wanadoo.fr
web	www.charm–hotel–paris.com

Carofftel Gobelins

18 avenue des Gobelins, 75005 Paris

Hidden between two restaurants, the Carofftel's canopy is easy to miss but once inside you will like the brand new, goldy-yellow entrance lounge which leads straight through into the pretty breakfast area with its tempting buffet at the back (cheese and ham, eggs and cereals...). Things are fairly diminutive here, apart from that view up the avenue (pictured: from streetside rooms on the higher floors) and the atmosphere is family-friendly yet respectful. Christine Caroff is bright and welcoming, she enjoys her life here and is ever helpful to guests. Leading off the deep salmon-pink and grey corridors, bedrooms are cheerfully pretty too – often sunny with lots of yellow, perhaps a blue or red patch or a softer oriental-style print. French country paintings – oils and watercolours – add individuality; beds are good; bathrooms may have old-fashioned tiling but are beautifully kept and the white laminated furniture is perfectly serviceable. So near the Latin Quarter and all its excitements, this is remarkable value – and very welcoming. *English spoken.*

rooms	23: 11 doubles, 6 twins/triples, 6 singles.
price	€57-€97.
meals	Buffet breakfast €8.
metro	Gobelins (7).
RER	Port Royal.
buses	27 47 83 91
car park	Patriarche.

Christine Caroff

tel	(0)1 42 17 47 47
fax	(0)1 42 17 47 30
e-mail	carofftel@adi.fr
web	hotelcarofftelgobelins.fr

The Gobelins tapestry workshops are a fiercely select, state-owned enterprise: there are just eight highly-skilled employees and they only accept commissions from the state.

map 4   entry 25

Hôtel Résidence Les Gobelins

9 rue des Gobelins, 75013 Paris

All here is quiet, attentive and unassuming – street, hotel, owners. And the patio is a real gift. Workers in the great Gobelins tapestry shops lived in this area and it was never very smart, but nearby is the entertaining, slightly bohemian Rue Mouffetard – little eating houses, big mosque, lively market and left-wing culture. The lounge, with country-cushioned wicker furniture, and the bright yellow, airy breakfast room decorated with much-loved black and white photographs of Paris and Parisians, lie round that honeysuckle-hung courtyard where guests can sit in peace. The rooms and bathrooms are simple, properly equipped – a writing table and chair, a decent cupboard and good towels – and have space (singles are small, of course, as are some doubles); décor is yellow, blue and grey, restful and harmonious. All rooms are quiet and light (though party walls may seem rather thin?). The Poiriers' gentle unobtrusive friendliness reminds the sensitive guest that the family used to keep a *pension de famille*; it has kept that incomparable sense of intimacy and understanding. *English and Spanish spoken.*

rooms	32: 10 singles, 14 doubles, 4 twins, 3 triples, 1 quadruple.
price	€ 55–€ 100.
meals	Breakfast € 7; lunch & dinner on request € 10–€ 30.
metro	Gobelins (7).
RER	Port Royal.
buses	27 47 83 91
car park	Place d'Italie.

In 1997, reconstruction works on the other side of the road revealed 12 5th-century stone sarcophagi containing coffin nails and skeletons, including one child and a horse.

Jennifer & Philippe Poirier

tel	(0)1 47 07 26 90
fax	(0)1 43 31 44 05
e-mail	hotelgobelins@noos.fr
web	hotelgobelins.com

Le Jardin de Cluny
9 rue Du Sommerard, 75005 Paris

In its quiet, friendly way and a variety of styles, this is a gently appealing place to stay run by a lively lady of knowledge. Full of light, the lobby is a mixture of 1980s gloss, neo-Assyrian ceramic bas-reliefs and comfortable yellow leather sitting corners. In the first-basement *salon-bar*, low brown/ginger armchairs and dusky mirrors create an intimate contemporary peace while the second-basement breakfast rooms feel thoroughly 17th century with their studded tapestry chairs and wall hangings under three stone vaults. On either side of the leafy green patio, bedrooms come in two buildings and two sorts – newer superior, older standard, both very pleasant though vibrant pink cotton, mushroom velours and dark wood furniture make the superiors look more modern, as do their very original bathrooms. But other, more traditional rooms dressed in bright prints and wicker furniture are good value, some have pretty new bathrooms and redecoration continues. Also, you can surf the net or send faxes from the little 'business corner' by the *salon*. A genuinely comfortable place so close to the Latin Quarter bustle. *English, German, Portuguese, Spanish spoken.*

rooms	40: 17 doubles, 15 twins, 6 singles, 1 triple, 1 quadruple.
price	€ 129–€ 244.
meals	Buffet breakfast € 11.
metro	Maubert-Mutualité (10).
RER	St Michel-Notre Dame (St Germain exit) (B, C).
buses	47 63 86 87
car park	Lagrange.

Madame Bauchet	
tel	(0)1 43 54 22 66
fax	(0)1 40 51 03 36
e-mail	hoteldecluny@wanadoo.fr
web	bw-paris-hotels.com/jardin

Some buildings on the Montagne Sainte Geneviève, the 'mountain' at the centre of medieval Paris, have all of seven basements (not all accessible nowadays), so two are really nothing to boast of.

map 4   entry 27

Hôtel La Tour Notre Dame
20 rue Du Sommerard, 75005 Paris

Two pillared emperors guard the *salon*, a large Greek urn waves its ferns, a medieval townscape hovers over the desk: ancient Greece and Rome are here, as well as Du Sommerard's beloved Middle Ages – the Cluny Medieval Museum does include the Roman baths of Lutetia (Roman Paris). You will be greeted by easy, helpful staff, many of whom have been here for years, headed by the delightful, youthful Catia. A tempting buffet breakfast is laid out in three stone vaults in the basement: attractive orange-tinted spaces with vanishing perspective murals (ancient Rome again) and solid Louis XIII chairs. Though not enormous, bedrooms have all the right bits of (French) Empire furniture and are all-over rich in fabric: dense Jouy country prints in thick raspberry, Mediterranean blue, dark mauve, or plain crimson with striped curtains – there is drama and intimacy in the air. In some, old beams and timbers add to the atmosphere. Bathrooms in classic grey marble or darker mosaic with elegant little friezes (and the occasional corner bath) finish the picture of a very quiet, welcoming, good-value place to stay in the Latin Quarter. *English spoken.*

In the 1830s, when the rest of the world swore only by Antiquity, Alexandre Du Sommerard collected medieval and Renaissance curiosities and treasures which became the bedrock of the Cluny Museum.

rooms	48: 20 doubles, 23 twins, 5 singles.
price	€ 119–€ 229.
meals	Buffet breakfast € 12.
metro	Cluny-La Sorbonne (10).
RER	St Michel-Notre Dame (St Germain exit).
buses	47 63 84 89
car park	Lagrange.

Catia Campoli

tel	(0)1 43 54 47 60
fax	(0)1 43 26 42 34
e-mail	tour-notre-dame@magic.fr
web	www.tour-notre-dame.com

Hôtel du Collège de France
7 rue Thénard, 75005 Paris

This hotel has an atmosphere of solid, well-established family comfort: exposed stones, lots of wood, soft armchairs by the fireplace in the red *salon*, good lighting. You will be greeted by the delightful young manager and by a less animated and considerably older Joan of Arc. The breakfast room is warmly red too, with old Parisian prints and a Madonna. Bedrooms are mostly not very big but each has a full-length mirror and a thoroughly practical desk unit. The décor is quite colourful in places with coordinated botanical fabrics, soft quilts – it is careful and restful, beds are new and bathrooms are fine. Some rooms have balconies over the street, rooms under the roof have beams and views, though you have to walk up from the fifth floor. But the staircase is worth visiting just for its round timbers and windows encrusted with autumn leaves. Several triple rooms and family apartments are possible and, above all, a genuinely friendly reception is assured. Excellent value on a quiet street away from the bustle of the main student drags – and you may receive useful intellectual vibrations from The Collège as a bonus. *English spoken.*

rooms	29: 23 doubles, 6 twins.
price	€ 70–€ 100.
meals	Unlimited continental breakfast € 7.
metro	St Michel (4), Maubert-Mutualité (10).
RER	St Michel-Notre Dame.
buses	21 24 27 38 63 85 86 87
car park	Maubert-Mutualité.

Jean & Laure Marc

tel	(0)1 43 26 78 36
fax	(0)1 46 34 58 29
e-mail	hotel.du.college.de.france@wanadoo.fr
web	hotel-collegedefrance.com

The Collège de France is an astonishing institution: lectures and courses by the greatest teachers and thinkers of the day are open to all, free of charge. Vive la France!

map 4   entry 29

Les Rives de Notre Dame
15 quai Saint Michel, 75005 Paris

With the colours and textures of the south and much imagination, an ancient Paris townhouse has become a very cosy hotel, in contrast to the severity of the police headquarters opposite. Only consider the darling lacey mimosa-encrusted petticoats that hang over the corridor windows, the minibar cupboards delicately painted by a brilliant Tuscan artisan, the 17th-century beams, the plants that rise to greet the light pouring in through the glass canopy. Through an arched 'fortress' door, each bedroom has its own combination of vibrantly sunny fabrics mixing flowers, stars and stripes, soft luxy duvets, head cushions on ivy-twined rods, a pretty bathroom and table and chairs for private breakfast, though the basement breakfast room is intimate and appealing too. Rooms are a good size (just three smaller first-floor rooms are given for singles but could take couples) and the top-floor studio is huge, if less recently furbished. Genuinely friendly and relaxed, your host has time to advise each guest on things to do. You should feel well cared for in this exceptional little house. (Good soundproofing against the traffic too.) *English, German, Italian spoken.*

Those bouquinistes on the embankment selling secondhand books of great or minimal value, old magazines and new postcards, are a radical Parisian institution who resist all attempts to 'organise' them.

rooms	10: 9 doubles/twins; 1 junior suite.
price	€ 168–€ 289; suite € 259–€ 381.
meals	Breakfast € 10.70–€ 13.70.
metro	St Michel (4).
RER	St Michel–Notre Dame.
buses	21 27 38 85 96
car park	Lutèce.

Danièle Limbert & Christian Martin

tel	(0)1 43 54 81 16
fax	(0)1 43 26 27 09
e-mail	hotel@rivesdenotredame.com
web	www.rivesdenotredame.com

Le Notre Dame Hôtel

1 quai Saint Michel, 75005 Paris

At the very hub of Latin Quarter life – students crowd the pavements, cars crowd the bridge, Notre Dame rises serene behind – you climb the mirrored staircase to a warm red welcome. The hotel is splendid: communal spaces brightly decked in red checks, the *salon*-breakfast room spreading its windows so your eyes are caught by plunging views of river, cathedral and great 'police palace'. Nearly all rooms have at least two windows onto this ancient picture; only the five cheapest, soberly pretty and quieter, give onto a dull courtyard. They are very attractive, not huge but uncluttered, and full of light from the river. Double-glazing keeps the noise out, air conditioning keeps the air breathable. Excellent fabrics are all from the house of Pierre Frey; a light cherry-wood laminate adorns desktops, bedheads and clever block panelling; there are hand-enamelled bedside lights from northern France and framed prints from England; new dark green marble bathrooms with bright white fittings are extremely smart behind their translucent Japanese-style doors and the top-floor duplex suites are fun and full of character. *English, German, Spanish spoken.*

rooms	26: 14 doubles, 9 twins; 3 duplex.
price	€ 150–€ 199; duplex € 244.
meals	Breakfast € 7.
metro	St Michel (4).
RER	St Michel-Notre Dame.
buses	24 47 63 86 87
car park	Notre Dame.

Monsieur Fouhety

tel	(0)1 43 54 20 43
fax	(0)1 43 26 61 75
e-mail	hotel.lenotredame@libertysurf.fr
web	www.lenotredamehotel.com/pages

Run out of bedtime reading? George Whitman's renowned Shakespeare & Co, American English-language bookshop and literary meeting place, is just down the road. Come for tea.

map 4   entry 31

Hôtel de la Sorbonne
6 rue Victor Cousin, 75005 Paris

Beneath the severe public face of the university, a secret hideaway. The door is at the back of a cobbled porchway and the hall huddles shyly behind a great fat pillar. In a quietly confidential atmosphere, an unusual antique kidney-shaped reception desk and a small leather sitting spot await you by the door; the delightful breakfast room beyond has the feel of a simple country-house morning room with its brick-red sponged walls, two bucket chairs beside the marble fireplace, high-backed wicker chairs and African animals in aged sepia ink to give proper psychological distance. Upstairs, corridors are tonic and appetising in leaf green and deep raspberry. The bedrooms, all being renovated, are not big, nor are the bath and shower rooms, but things are kept simple and uncluttered: white piqué bedcovers, a different colour theme on each floor – mauve or green or blue, simple wooden bedheads, good-quality mattresses, pale stripey wallpapers and bathrooms in either good, new or rather old-fashioned but perfectly adequate tiles; good mirrors too. A quiet, nicely-done hotel in a superb position. *English, German and Spanish spoken.*

rooms	37: 29 doubles, 8 twins.
price	€80–€90.
meals	Breakfast €5.
metro	Cluny-La Sorbonne (10).
RER	Luxembourg, St Michel-Notre Dame.
buses	21 27 38 63 82 84 86 97
car park	Rue Soufflot.

The centre of academic excellence founded in 1257 by Robert de Sorbon was initially called the Community of Poor Masters and Theological Students. How things change.

Frédéric Lopez

tel	(0)1 43 54 58 08
fax	(0)1 40 51 05 18
e-mail	reservation@hotelsorbonne.com
web	www.hotelsorbonne.com

Hôtel des Trois Collèges

16 rue Cujas, 75005 Paris

The open, welcoming ground floor of the hotel is your breakfast room and, occasionally, a tea room doing light lunches for all comers or private parties. Busy people rush past the big windows but a properly academic atmosphere reigns in the pale and tranquil interior, though the reception bustles at peak hours. The walls are hung with portraits of some great old names of knowledge and with ancient plans showing the Latin Quarter through the ages: the building's foundations were probably laid when Lutetia was capital of Roman Gaul. In a corner by the lobby, the 22-metre well still holds water: for centuries, it was the single source of water for the two buildings round the little courtyard. Bedrooms are simple with lots of white furniture and pretty pastel-hued piqué bedcovers. The second pillow is dressed up as a cushion on top, there are splashes of colours in the curtains, good functional bathrooms have all essentials plus a clothes line. It is a very pleasant and reasonable place to stay right beneath the looming wall of the Sorbonne where tomorrow's leaders are as yet learning their future trades. *English and German spoken.*

rooms	44: 27 doubles, 5 twins, 10 singles, 2 triples.
price	€65-€135.
meals	Breakfast €7.
metro	Cluny-La Sorbonne (10).
RER	Luxembourg, St Michel-Notre Dame.
buses	21 27 38 63 82 84 86 87
car park	Rue Soufflot.

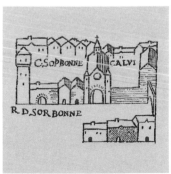

Madame Wyplosz

tel	(0)1 43 54 67 30
fax	(0)1 46 34 02 99
e-mail	hotel@3colleges.com
web	www.3colleges.com

Victor Cousin, an ambitious philosopher who worked hard to combine Descartes, Kant and the Scottish school in one great eclectic system, left this thought: It is better to have a future than a past.

map 4   entry 33

Hôtel Le Clos Médicis

56 rue Monsieur le Prince, 75006 Paris

The display in the old shop window is always high fashion; when you come in from the noisy, excited Boulevard St Michel you will hear muted jazz, feel soft air. In this place of quiet contemporary class, the attractive countersunk *salon* has a welcoming fire, deep brown armchairs, jungle pictures and a fine stone pillar; beyond it are the sunny Tuscan patio and the delightful young team at reception. To ground its very Parisian personality, the Médicis has opted for roots in provincial soil: a *clos* is a vineyard and each room is named after a famous wine. Bedrooms have been redesigned by fashionable names in strong silent colours – rich red and blue, white, ginger and brown – real fabrics with wide contrasting borders, big deep-framed mirrors and natural-sophisticated wildlife prints. One room has a private terrace, another is a nicely-arranged duplex; all are soundproofed and, if not always very big, are extremely comfortable. Bathrooms are still impeccable, the tiling brings a whiff of Provence, the details have all been thought through. Add that lively sense of hospitality – it's excellent. *English, Spanish and Italian spoken.*

The Mr Prince here was a powerful Bourbon who nevertheless had to whisk his bride away from Paris straight after their wedding in 1609 to remove her from the King's over-pressing attentions.

rooms	38: 16 doubles, 20 doubles/twins, 1 triple, 1 duplex.
price	€ 135–€ 240.
meals	Generous buffet breakfast € 11.
metro	Odéon (4, 10).
RER	Luxembourg.
buses	21 38 82 84 85 89
car park	Rue Soufflot.

Olivier Méallet

tel	(0)1 43 29 10 80
fax	(0)1 43 54 26 90
e-mail	message@closmedicis.com
web	www.closmedicis.com

Hôtel Saint Paul Rive Gauche

43 rue Monsieur le Prince, 75006 Paris

Sheer bliss to step out of the battle between cars and pedestrians into this civilised house, wrapped in layers of quiet left by the Franciscans who once lived here. A long beamed hall looks past antiques and tapestries, tooled Spanish leather and wrought iron, to a tiny patio full of flowers and light. Four generations of a Franco-British family have made the St Paul a marriage of French elegance and English comfort – Indian rugs here and there, decorative cast-iron firebacks (Madame's passion), and Hugo the loving Labrador. The attractive *salon*, lit by a fine painting of giant sunflowers and a big window, has a piano and rather theatrical wall drapery; the breakfast room is wonderfully medieval with its stone vault, ancient well and high tapestried chairs – modernity taking the shape of designer reeds and a generous cooked breakfast. Bedrooms come in different sizes, colours and furnishings – some quite small, junior suites a decent size, lots of warm yellows and reds, nice old pieces of furniture, good little bathrooms – and staff are lively, welcoming and... relaxed. *Air conditioning in some rooms. English, Italian, Spanish, Swedish spoken.*

rooms	31: 21 doubles, 7 twins, 3 junior suites for 4. Connecting rooms.
price	€ 112–€ 158, suites € 174–€ 204.
meals	Breakfast € 10–€ 13.
metro	Odéon (4, 10).
RER	Luxembourg.
buses	38 63 82 85 86 87 95 96
car park	Rue Soufflot.

Marianne Oberlin

tel	(0)1 43 26 98 64
fax	(0)1 46 34 58 60
e-mail	hotel.saint.paul@wanadoo.fr

Parts of King Philippe Auguste's vast city walls can be seen here. We know him as the conqueror of bad King John 'Lackland' of England who lost Normandy to him in 1204.

map 4   entry 35

MONTPARNASSE - LUXEMBOURG

Hannibal - Hell - Seminary - Eternal Youth

Hôtel Aiglon

232 boulevard Raspail, 75014 Paris

The imperial eagle (see below) flies over the generous spaces of the Aiglon, depositing Empire furniture, an Empire lift, an Empire bar... The atmosphere of rich colours, sobriety and confidence is very relaxing. The next delight is the large, light mahogany-panelled breakfast room on the first floor looking over the trees. Every bedroom has a lobby, a walk-in cupboard and custom-made, Empire-style furniture; mostly big by Paris standards, they are supremely restful in green and yellow or deep beige with soft prints; carpets are gentle grey and brown; fine table lamps by Drimmer and watercolours add grace; firm new mattresses guarantee comfort. In the light-tiled well-equipped bathrooms, even the small shower rooms have proper stalls. Many rooms give onto tree-lined avenues whence most traffic disappears at night, and some receive the green peace of the cemetery. The superb deluxe suite is imperially vast and its minibar has columns – but the welcome is by no means haughtily Empire or powerfully Napoleonic. People stay for weeks, come again and often become friends of this warm family. *Internet access. English spoken.*

rooms	47: 30 doubles, 8 twins, 8 suites, 1 apartment for 4.
price	€ 107–€ 142; suites € 179; apartment € 244.
meals	Breakfast € 7.
metro	Raspail (4).
RER	Et Orlybus: Denfert Rochereau.
buses	68 91
car park	Hotel or Edgar Quinet.

Jacques Rols

tel	(0)1 43 20 82 42
fax	(0)1 43 20 98 72
e-mail	hotelaiglon@wanadoo.fr

Napoleon's son and heir, nicknamed Aiglon (Little Eagle), died at 21 and never carried the Imperial insignia. The previous owner of the hotel was an ardent fan of Napoleon.

map 4   entry 36

Hôtel Istria

29 rue Campagne Première, 75014 Paris

You will receive a genuine welcome from Daniel Crétey at the Istria, so well placed for airports, mainline stations and lively Montparnasse yet secluded in a quiet back street. A haunt of the wild arty avant-garde who lived, loved and worked here in the 1930s, the hotel now promises peace and quiet with its deep leather sofas and tartan chairs, celebrity reduced to a small wooden Charlie Chaplin sitting benignly in the corner. Plain, simple, good-quality furnishings and décor are the hallmark: the modern bedroom furniture made of gently-curved and rounded pieces of solid elm, specially designed for the Istria, is enlivened with fine-checked or striped fabrics and heavy stainless steel table lamps. The same discreet, simple taste prevails in the palest yellow Korean grass wallpaper. The showers (there are four baths in all) are delightful quarter-circle constructions, beds have slatted bases, mattresses are firm new Dunlopillo. In the lovely stone-vaulted breakfast room soft lighting lifts the scattered yellow and orange flowers from the tablecloths. Charm and thoroughly good value for two stars near Montparnasse. *English spoken.*

rooms	26: 17 doubles, 9 twins.
price	€92–€100.
meals	Continental-plus breakfast €8.
metro	Raspail (4, 6).
RER	Port-Royal.
buses	68 91
car park	Montparnasse.

The Istria was immortalised by Louis Aragon in a poem to his beloved Elsa; Duchamp invented his 'readymade' art here; Man Ray took pictures - enough glory?

Daniel Crétey

tel	(0)1 43 20 91 82
fax	(0)1 43 22 48 45
e-mail	istria@wanadoo.fr
web	www.360degrees.com

Hôtel Raspail Montparnasse
203 boulevard Raspail, 75014 Paris

Below the satisfyingly genuine 1924 frontage, the heavy old doors spring towards you as you approach – 1990s magic. There's old-style generosity in the high Art Deco lobby with its ceiling fans, bucket chairs and play of squares and curves. In the bedrooms, 1930s or modern furniture sits well with pale unfussy quilts, pretty lamps and elegant curtain fabric. To each floor a colour: quiet grey, sunny ochre, powder-puff blue; to each landing a matching stained glass window – good additions to the original 1920s framework. Obviously, the higher the price, the bigger the room, but even the 'standard' has a decent desk and an armchair while 'superiors' are most attractive and stylishly white-tiled, colour-friezed bathrooms have smart matt washbasins. Rooms are named after famous Montparnasse artists and each one is hung with an appropriate reproduction; some have the added perk of an Eiffel Tower view. Montparnasse still bustles crazily down below and a friendly, lively and efficient welcome is the first and final flourish. *NB. Don't confuse it with the Mercure Raspail Montparnasse two doors down. English, German, Italian and Spanish spoken.*

rooms	38: 18 doubles, 13 twins, 5 singles, 2 suites.
price	€96-€162, suites €199.
meals	Breakfast €9
metro	Vavin (4), Raspail (4, 6).
RER	Port Royal.
buses	58 68 82 91
car park	Montparnasse-Raspail.

Madame Christiane Martinent

tel	(0)1 43 20 62 86
fax	(0)1 43 20 50 79
e-mail	raspailm@wanadoo.fr
web	www.charming-hotel-paris.com

That statue of Balzac, author of the immense Comédie Humaine, by the equally famous sculptor Rodin, shocked contemporaries who saw it as 'a madman in his dressing-gown'.

map 4   entry 38

Le Royal Luxembourg

212 boulevard Raspail, 75014 Paris

The cool, clear lines and colours of designer Jean-Philippe Nuel's interior bathe you in white and mauve, brown and crimson as soon as you enter the big airy lobby to be greeted by the eager young owner or his team. Then there are the ultra-fashionable stiff moiré curtains and modern flower statements with the baroque contrast of leafy prints on the sitting-room walls. The same generous sense of space fills the coir-floored breakfast room beneath its glass canopy: wicker armchairs, dark modern furniture, mauve, white and pink cloths, Bakst's wonderful costume designs for Diaghilev. Just enough of everything. The bedrooms are done in quiet colours too – mushroom, yellow or dark raspberry – with big padded headboards, good repro furniture, adequate storage and, mostly, decent amounts of space. You will find the bathrooms in keeping: all newly-tiled, they have marble tops, excellent fittings and heated towel rails. There's a lot of activity down on the crossroads – you are near Montparnasse's immortal cafés – but the Royal Luxembourg is a place for quiet retirement before you launch into the excitement. *English and Italian spoken.*

rooms	48: 24 doubles, 15 twins, 2 singles, 7 triples.
price	€ 120–€ 200, including breakfast.
meals	Buffet breakfast included.
metro	Vavin (4), Raspail (12, 13).
RER	Port Royal, Denfert Rochereau.
buses	68 91
car park	Boulevard Montparnasse.

In the 1930s, the hotel had a restaurant and was a favourite haunt of the Anglo-American literary scene - Lawrence Durrell, Ernest Hemingway and Arthur Miller called it 'Le Petit Ritz'.

Monsieur Ouassini

tel	(0)1 43 20 69 20
fax	(0) 42 79 95 23
e–mail	hotel.leroyal@wanadoo.fr
web	www.hotelleroyal.com

Hôtel Jardin Le Bréa

14 rue Bréa, 75006 Paris

Live plants are restricted to the little conservatory but the inside is all as pretty as a garden, without being oversweet or cloying, and if you find the soft brick and yellow sitting room by the entrance attractive, then try the open-table bar space by the skylit conservatory – it's adorable in its crimson and gold finery, wicker chairs and orchids, not to mention Hilton McConnico's petal picture. The new young owner has a flair for interiors and guided designer Nuel into producing a very personal expression of her own ideas and space. Upstairs (there are two buildings), you find colourful corridors – in red, yellow and duck green – leading to pretty feminine bedrooms and perfect little bathrooms. She has done it all in three basic colour schemes: blue, red and green, all backed onto yellow. There are friezes round the walls, pleasing contemporary fabrics with coordinated edgings, cane furniture or modern takes on Louis XVI; limited space is well used. Warm embracing colours, a young feminine presence and a welcoming atmosphere – what more can you want? *No lift in second building (two floors). English and Spanish spoken.*

rooms	25: 16 doubles, 8 twins, 1 single.
price	€ 120–€ 155.
meals	Buffet breakfast € 10.
metro	Vavin (4).
RER	Port Royal.
buses	58 68 82 91
car park	Boulevard Montparnasse.

Madame Faïza Ouassini	
tel	(0)1 43 25 44 41
fax	(0)1 44 07 19 25
e-mail	brea.hotel@wanadoo.fr
web	www.jardinlebrea-paris-hotel.com

Not a poetic, peaceful or Parnassian story, that of General Bréa: during the 1848 revolution, he went to negotiate with a group of insurgents at Fontainebleau and was promptly assassinated.

map 4   entry 40

Le Sainte Beuve

9 rue Sainte Beuve, 75006 Paris

This beautifully refurbished hotel, known and loved during the wilder days of Montparnasse, now exudes an atmosphere of unstuffy designer luxury – quiet good taste in gentle tones and thick fabrics. The extraordinarily attractive *salon* has superb silk curtains, a winter log fire in the old marble fireplace, modern paintings and old prints. It is all small and intimate and the attentive, efficient staff are a vital element in your sense of wellbeing here. Bedrooms are intimate too in ancient and modern finery: lots of pale walls, soft colours and textured fabrics, colourful chintzes and paisleys modulated by pastels, at least one antique per room – a leather-topped desk, a walnut dressing-table, a polished *armoire*, old brass lamps – and 18th/19th-century pictures in rich old frames. The special *Sainte Beuve* room is extra-big and in dazzling good taste. Bathrooms are superbly modern with bathrobes and fine toiletries. Lastly, for the first moments of the day, breakfast is a feast of croissants and brioches from the famous Mulot bakery and fresh orange juice. *English spoken. Round-the-clock internet access. Book early.*

Moral philosopher and literary critic, Sainte Beuve was known for his bons mots such as "The historian is a prophet of the past", "So many die before meeting themselves".

rooms	22: 7 doubles, 15 twins, including *Sainte Beuve* room.
price	€126–€225; *Sainte Beuve* €265.
meals	Breakfast €13.50; lunch & dinner on request €7–€30.
metro	Notre Dame des Champs (12), Vavin (4).
RER	Port-Royal.
buses	48 58 82 89 91 92 94 95 96
car park	Montparnasse.

Jean-Pierre Egurreguy

tel	(0)1 45 48 20 07
fax	(0)1 45 48 67 52
e-mail	saintebeuve@wanadoo.fr
web	www.paris-hotel-charme.com

Pension Les Marronniers
78 rue d'Assas, 75006 Paris

It's an honest-to-goodness *pension de famille*, one of the last – down from 400 to six in Paris since 1970 – so if you're young and penniless or old and nostalgic, make the most of Marie's quintessentially French family place overlooking the Luxembourg Gardens. It's been her family's *pension* since the 1930s and is as personal and cluttered as anything in Balzac. There are countless pictures, portraits and photographs, there are statues and plants galore, notices for inmates on flower pots and mantelpieces, a cuckoo clock that was silenced 20 years ago and a superbly carved, grass-green country *armoire* topped with a motley crew of candlesticks. Marie coddles her guests (some have been here for years) and loves cooking for them: she clearly enjoys food herself and makes sure others do too. She is also down to-earth, compassionate, perceptive and hard working - a remarkable woman. The bedrooms for short-stayers have less personality than the dining and drawing rooms, rather as if they have been furnished with what was left over, and most share washing facilities. But what counts is the wonderful welcome, the tradition and the food. *English spoken.*

rooms	12: some with own shower & wc, some sharing.
price	Half-board €27–€62.
meals	Breakfast included. Dinner included except Sundays (brunch on Saturdays); vegetarian dishes on request.
metro	Notre Dame des Champs (12), Vavin (4).
RER	Luxembourg.
buses	58 82 83
car park	Rue Auguste Comte

Marie Poirier

tel	(0)1 43 26 37 71
fax	(0)1 43 26 07 72
e-mail	o_marro@club-internet.fr
web	www.pension-marronniers.com

Legend has it that Captain Assus of the Auvergne Chasseurs, while searching a wood alone one night, was taken by the enemy and died while saving his comrades by shouting "À moi l'Auvergne!"

map 4   entry 42

Hôtel Le Saint Grégoire

43 rue de l'Abbé Grégoire, 75006 Paris

There's genuine 18th-century style in the tall slim façade – forget the uglies opposite. Inside, the elegance is period pink yet warmly 20th century: deep comfortable chairs, Indian rugs on fitted carpets and a David Hicks-designed décor in plum, old pink and ginger with stripey half-curtains, a simple classical fireplace (fires in winter), portraits of 'other people's cousins', a little reading corner with button chairs. The welcome is friendly, attentive and intelligent in a gentle atmosphere of quiet classical music and antiques lovingly collected by the owners. In one room you will find a set of intriguing folding coathooks, in another an unusual thickset writing desk that bears witness to some serious work. Room sizes vary but every one has a genuinely old piece or two. Pinks, browns and white are the colours, including bathroom marble and pretty rugs strewn everywhere. The rooms over the street are the larger, some with two windows, but breakfast on a private terrace is perhaps the tops. Serene, intimate and utterly French, it is linked to the larger Tourville and Lavoisier hotels. *English, German, Italian, Spanish spoken.*

Abbé Grégoire was a revolutionary bishop who proposed ending the feudal Right of Primogeniture (eldest boy takes all) and got France to abolish slavery in 1794.

rooms	20: 10 doubles, 9 twins, 1 junior suite.
price	€175–€248.
meals	Continental-plus breakfast €12.
metro	St Placide (4), Sèvres-Babylone (10, 12).
RER	Luxembourg.
buses	63 68 84 89 92 94
car park	Opposite hotel.

Michel Bouvier & François de Bené

tel	(0)1 45 48 23 23
fax	(0)1 45 48 33 95
e-mail	hotel@saintgregoire.com
web	www.hotelsaintgregoire.com

Hôtel Ferrandi
92 rue du Cherche Midi, 75006 Paris

Behind that rhythmic and harmonious façade (every room looks this way), you will find a cheerful, efficient team and superb old-style French refinement. Some of the beautiful antiques in the *salon* are family pieces, each fabric, flounce and swag, every 1920s poster, print and drawing has been lovingly chosen to delight your eye and the club like breakfast room is properly intimate behind its screen of greenery. Enter the smallest room: a deeply tempting dark blue and white nest lined with quiet scenes of Ancient Greece and enfolding a pure white brass-headed bed in a soft ivory alcove with every detail perfect. The very generous deluxe rooms are variously decked in wine red, rich blue or salmon pink Jouy print of romantic country scenes with matching plush chairs and a big desk each. Curtains are luxuriously thick, bathrooms dressed in marble slabs or good tiles, Other careful details: good sound-proofing, excellent tap fittings, interactive film/TV system: they want you to feel absolutely at home in this place of rich peace and proper comfort. *English, German, Italian and Spanish spoken.*

rooms	42: 41 doubles/twins, 1 suite for 4. Connecting rooms.
price	€ 106-€ 220; suite € 260.
meals	Continental-plus breakfast € 10.
metro	Vaneau (10), St Placide (4).
RER	St Michel-Notre Dame
buses	39 95 40 82 68 70
car park	Consult hotel.

Madame Lafond

tel	(0)1 42 22 97 40
fax	(0)1 45 44 89 97
e-mail	hotel.ferrandi@wanadoo.fr

The street was named in 1595, in the days when a cherche-midi was a social parasite who made a habit of visiting at noon in the hope of being invited to lunch at 12.30.

map 3   entry 44

Hôtel Mayet

3 rue Mayet, 75006 Paris

Youthful and fun, the Mayet is as light-hearted and comfortable as a new makeover could concoct: Laurence Raymond's love of life is evident at every turn. On the delectable old oak lobby floor, the desk is an office unit lookalike with two black meeting-room lamps overhead, the internet point is a brilliant red iron biped with a one-legged steel stool for surfers. To left and right, two graffiti artists have been at bright, drippy mural work, the deep sofas are richly natural, the venetian blinds softly luminous. Here reigns warm, smiling Roselie: she's been at the Mayet for years and delights in its brave new look. Walk down to breakfast: every step is carpeted a different, vibrant colour; the stone vault houses a trio of self-service shelves and one long colourful table on a stripey floor. In cafeteria style, you can even choose the colour of your mug – and spoil your partner by taking them breakfast in bed. Bedrooms are all as illustrated, in grey, white and dark red, with 'office' furniture, good little bathrooms and excellent bedding. But each room number is an original piece of art. As we said, huge fun. *Internet access. English spoken.*

For five centuries, the Rue de Sèvres was a country lane leading from Paris to a modest village across the river called - Sèvres. Then porcelain-making fame rose in 1764 and modesty sank without trace.

rooms	23: 17 doubles, 4 twins, 1 triple, 1 single.
price	€ 100–€ 140 including breakfast.
meals	Self-service breakfast included.
metro	Duroc (10, 13), Vaneau (10).
RER	Montparnasse.
buses	28 39 70 82 87 89 92
car park	Montparnasse.

Laurence Raymond & Roselie	
tel	(0)1 47 83 21 35
fax	(0)1 40 65 95 78
e-mail	hotel@mayet.com
web	www.mayet.com

Hôtel Apollon Montparnasse
91 rue de l'Ouest/54 rue Pernety, 75014 Paris

Light pours into the flame-coloured lobby from the two streets that meet here – two quietish little streets in this old-style backwater where a slower pace reigns and the metropolitan hubbub seems miles away: there should be little traffic at night. The Prigents named their hotel on the Parisian Parnassus after meeting Apollo on the Roman Parnassus but have not yet found his likeness, even on trips to Greece. And no Ionic scrolls or Corinthian curls either· this is a simple place to stay. Rooms are all furnished in pale laminated wood, clean and neat, with orange papered walls and either brick-coloured or green and ochre fabrics of contemporary quality. The quilted bedcovers are bright and welcoming, bathrooms are coolly grey and fully equipped and only the single rooms are really small. Breakfast is in the vaulted basement where discreet lighting and modern furniture set off the old stones. The Apollon is sound value in a lesser-known Parisian 'village' where shopping is fun – little old shops that appear not to have changed for 50 years alongside the Rue d'Alésia whose discount outlets draw thousands. *English, German, Portuguese and Spanish spoken.*

rooms	33: 23 doubles, 4 twins, 5 singles, 1 triple.
price	€ 66–€ 80.
meals	Breakfast € 6.20.
metro	Pernety (13).
RER	Denfert Rochereau.
buses	28 58 68 92
car park	Consult hotel.

Dom Antoine Pernety was an 18th-century monk who spent years searching for the philosopher's stone and the elixir of eternal life. He died, unsuccessful we conclude, at 85 and a pauper.

Isabelle & Hervé Prigent

tel	(0)1 43 95 62 00
fax	(0)1 43 95 62 10
e-mail	apollonm@wanadoo.fr
web	www.apollon-montparnasse.com

map 3   entry 46

ST GERMAIN DES PRÉS - ORSAY

Rue des Quatre Vents
Rue de l'Hirondelle
Rue de la Chaise

Four Winds - Swallow - Chair

Hôtel des Écoles

19 rue Monsieur le Prince, 75006 Paris

The lobby is superbly generous for such a modest hotel: the piano, the utterly French antiques on the dark wooden floor, the Regency stripes at the window are all shades of old family houses. And guests are received in appropriately relaxed and courteous manner by the new owners. You can even look forward to candlelit breakfast beneath the old stone vault hung with Moroccan rugs – eat as many croissants as you like, it's entirely self service. Bedrooms are somewhat different. Small, of course, bright and variegated, they have had less work done on them for the moment; several even have a fold-down couchette over the main bed for an extra child in an emergency and what must be the first ever 'power showers', looking like pieces of industrial plumbing and highly effective. Colours are light, there are pretty fabrics with little flowers, big flowers, checks and stripes. The triple on the top floor is bigger, richly red and ginger, with a gauzy canopy over the antique bed (pictured). Courtyard rooms are darker but slightly larger than streetside rooms and the compact little bathrooms are all perfectly adequate. Great value. *Arabic, English and Italian spoken.*

rooms	11: 10 doubles/twins, 1 triple.
price	€79–€129.
meals	Continental buffet breakfast €8
metro	Odéon (4, 10).
RER	St Michel-Notre Dame.
buses	58 63 86 87 96
car park	Rue de l'École de Médecine.

Monsieur Imed & Monsieur Redha

tel	(0)1 46 33 31 69
fax	(0)1 43 26 30 04
e-mail	hotel_des_ecoles@hotmail.com
web	www.hoteldesecoles.com

The Prince of Condé bought a mansion here in 1612 with compensation money given by Louis XIII for the loss of a very lucrative commission when he had to flee the King's father's lustful designs on his young bride.

map 4   entry 47

Grand Hôtel des Balcons

3 rue Casimir Delavigne, 75006 Paris

*L*es *Balcons* has the lot: an idea of service which produces tea on winter afternoons, a clothes line over the bath, a practical room where clients can work or children play, a daily feast of a breakfast (sumptuous cooked spread, fresh fruit salad…) that's free on your birthday! Owners and staff appear to work with lightness and pleasure. Having decorated her Art Nouveau hotel by taking inspiration from the floral delights of the original 1890s staircase windows, Denise Corroyer now teaches *ikebana* and flowers the house – brilliantly – while her son Jeff manages – charmingly. Rooms are simple yet pleasing. The five big family rooms have smart décor and pretty modern lamps, parquet floors and two windows, good bathrooms (two basins, pretty tiles) and loads of space. Other rooms are not big but purpose-made table units use the space judiciously, amusing prints decorate the walls and front rooms have balconies. At the back, you may be woken by the birds. An eagle eye is kept and no damage left unrepaired, beds are firm, bathrooms good, colours and fabrics simple and pleasantly bright. Remarkable value, super people. *English and Spanish spoken.*

rooms	50: 25 doubles, 14 twins, 6 singles, 5 family rooms for 4.
price	€72–€180.
meals	Superb buffet breakfast €10.
metro	Odéon (4, 10).
RER	Luxembourg.
buses	24 63 86 87 96
car park	École de Médecine.

The classical-fronted Odéon, Second National Theatre 150 years ago, which closed down in 1968 for allowing students to preach revolution on the stage, is again sagely part of the Comédie Française.

Denise & Pierre Corroyer & Jeff André

tel	(0)1 46 34 /8 50
fax	(0)1 46 34 06 27
e-mail	resa@balcons.com
web	www.balcons.com

Hôtel Louis II

2 rue Saint-Sulpice, 75006 Paris

Welcoming? The smell of fresh toast travels up to you in the morning. Quirky? All beds have been adjusted to the uneven old floors. Charming? Imagination has triumphed in this 18th-century house, often to dramatic effect, so that even the smallest rooms (some are very snug) have huge personality. Two have dazzling wraparound *trompe-l'œil* pictures set into the timber frame. On the top floor, you sleep under ancient sloping roof rafters in a long flower-papered room with an old rustic *armoire* or a 1920s cheval glass. One bathroom has brass taps and a yellow cockleshell basin, the other has an oval bath and burnished copper fittings. Every room is different, sheets are floral and match the décor, bath/shower rooms are small but fully equipped. Descend to a generous and refined breakfast in the golden elegance of the big *salon* with its magnificent fanning beams and superb double-sided curtains. Gilt-framed mirrors, fine antiques and candelabras complete the picture. You will be enthusiastically welcomed here and properly cared for: attention to detail is essential and they tend to treat guests like visiting friends. English spoken.

rooms	22: 17 doubles, 3 twins, 2 triples.
price	€120–€230; child under 3 free.
meals	Breakfast €9–€14.
metro	Odéon (4, 10).
RER	St Michel-Notre Dame.
buses	63 87 86 96 50 70
car park	St Sulpice.

François Meynant

tel	(0)1 46 33 13 80
fax	(0)1 46 33 17 29
e-mail	louis2@club-internet.fr
web	www.hotel-louis2.com

Prince Louis II was the Grand Condé who fought so brilliantly first against, then for, King Louis XIV then retired in peace and wealth to Chantilly, surrounded by great writers and poets.

map 4   entry 49

Hôtel du Globe

15 rue des Quatre-Vents, 75006 Paris

Closed in August. Miniature is the word, for the hotel, the rooms, the staircase, the storage, but huge are the hearts of the small team who run it. They adore their little hostelry, put fresh flowers in your room and want only that you adore it too. Greet the iron man, walk up the stairs and you will find the *Réception*: a sitting room full of furniture and papers, no office machines – you are in someone's house and they welcome you with a smile rather than a form to fill in. Bedcovers are grandmotherly crochet, there are beams, old stones and four-posters, pink rooms and yellow rooms, little carved *guéridon* tables, tiny folding writing tables and dozens of bits and pieces. Even the drinks list in your bedroom is hand written. The smallest have shower, basin and loo neatly hidden behind cupboard doors hand-painted by a skilful artist. Rooms with baths are larger but breakfast is brought to your room, whatever its size. For character, charm and warmth of welcome, the Globe is hard to beat. A warning to light sleepers: take earplugs in case you are in a streetside (disco-side) room: this is living Paris. *English, German and Spanish spoken.*

In the 17th century, the four winds (Quatre Vents) blew to the four corners of the earth from the round cheeks and delicious lips of four cherubs - on a shop sign.

rooms	15 doubles.
price	€ 66–€ 100.
meals	Breakfast € 8.
metro	Odéon (4, 10).
RER	Cluny-La Sorbonne.
buses	86 87
car park	St Sulpice.

Simonne Ressier

tel	(0)1 46 33 62 69/(0)1 43 26 35 50
fax	(0)1 46 33 62 69

Hôtel de l'Odéon

13 rue Saint Sulpice, 75006 Paris

Beyond the smartly spreading new frontage is a feast of elegance, oak panelling and attention to detail round a tiny planted light well and a hand-made, antique-fitted glass telephone box. The splendid new red *salon* invites you to croissants in comfort or newspaper lazing by the light of its old bronze lamps while the antique beds upstairs would make any collector envious. You may have a canopied four-poster (or two), or a pair of elaborately decorated cast-iron beds, accompanied by crochet bedcovers, a nice old mirror, a window onto the narrow street or greenery. Beams teem, carefully-coordinated colour schemes convey a sense of quiet traditional comfort and bathrooms are marble. The owner has used his ingenuity and sense of architectural volumes to make even the small rooms feel special (e.g. two windows cantilevered over the patio transforming a narrow cell into a real single). Wherever feasible, those antique bedsteads have been adapted to take extra-wide mattresses. The Odéon is quiet and friendly and there's space to move. Room arrangements are variable and most requests can be met so do ask when booking. *Internet access. English spoken.*

rooms	30: 18 doubles, 8 twins, 4 family rooms for 3-5.
price	€ 145–€ 270.
meals	Buffet breakfast € 11.
metro	Odéon (1, 10).
RER	St Michel-Notre Dame.
buses	21 27 38 58 82 84 85 89
car park	St Sulpice.

Monsieur & Madame Pilfert

tel	(0)1 43 25 70 11
fax	(0)1 43 29 97 34
e-mail	hotelodeon@wanadoo.fr
web	www.paris-hotel-odeon.com

The secular astronomical Gnomon in St Sulpice catches sunlight from a hole in the wall and projects it onto the brass line inlaid in the floor to announce equinoxes and solstices.

map 4   entry 51

Hôtel le Clément
6 rue Clément, 75006 Paris

This delightful little hotel has been in the same family for 100 years and Madame Charrade, the fourth generation, is the gentlest professional hotelier you could hope to meet. Charming and communicative, she takes care of her guests like family. From the higher floors, the view across the (sadly modernised) St Germain marketplace to the towers of St Sulpice Church is super and rooms at the top have loads of character with their sloping ceilings, if somewhat less space. Back rooms have no view, of course, except over the pretty planted space at the bottom of one of the lightwells (the hotel occupies two connecting buildings), but peace is guaranteed here. Madame's decorative style is southern cottage: small spriggy or floral prints, harmonious wallpapers, good colour combinations — brick-red and mustard, midnight blue and ivory, Provençal red and orange — and white piqué bedcovers; bathrooms are often tiled in colourful mosaic and renovations are always under way. The big ground-floor breakfast room, formerly the restaurant, is due to be redone with panelling, bookshelves and wicker furniture. A place of welcome and good value. *English spoken.*

rooms	25: 11 doubles, 6 twins, 5 triples, 3 suites for three.
price	€ 105–€ 123, suites € 123–€ 138.
meals	Buffet breakfast € 10.
metro	Mabillon (10), St Germain des Prés (4).
RER	Luxembourg.
buses	63 70 85 86 95 96
car park	Opposite hotel.

Dom François Clément was a bookish historian whose only claim to fame seems to have been his skill at finishing other people's books: Clémencet's How to Check Dates, Bouquet's Historians of Gaul and France...

Monsieur & Madame Charrade

tel	(0)1 43 26 53 60
fax	(0)144 07 06 83
e-mail	hclement@worldnet.fr
web	www.hotel-clement.com

Hôtel Perreyve

63 rue Madame, 75006 Paris

Afew steps from the oh-so-Parisian Luxembourg Gardens, 10 minutes from St Germain des Prés, the Perreyve has an enchanting face lidded by an old glass awning. Admire the glazier's curvaceous art in the elegant front door: there are several of these original gems as well as an attractive, family-comfortable blue-plush *salon* where guests can sit and read in peace and tables are set for breakfast, then cleared to leave the antique wood glowing. Two magnificent plants prove that living things thrive here. The calm and collected owners have been here for years, love their wonderful Left Bank and are quietly settled in their ways and means. Plain and simple bedrooms, giving onto one of two peaceful streets or the narrow courtyard, have all sorts of layouts and colours. There's a single with two windows and balconies: masses of view, little floor space; a double with a vertical roof timber in the middle; beige wallpapers, 1980s laminated furniture, oldish showers and some bright splashes. But come for the surroundings, the *salon* and the quiet welcome, not for fabulous finishes or design. *English and Spanish spoken.*

rooms	31: 17 doubles, 10 twins, 3 singles, 1 triple.
price	€89-€136.
meals	Breakfast €8.
metro	St Placide (4).
RER	Luxembourg.
buses	58 83 89
car park	Place St Sulpice.

Monsieur Doumergue

tel	(0)1 45 48 35 01
fax	(0)1 45 48 35 01
e-mail	perreyve@club-internet.fr
web	www.hotelperreyve.com

The more aristocratic you were, the simpler your title: not surprisingly, Madame was the wife of Monsieur... younger brother of Louis XVI. Her full name? Marie Josephine Louise of Savoy, Princess of Sardinia.

map 4   entry 53

Hôtel de Buci

22 rue Buci, 75006 Paris

At the heart of the little shopping streets behind St Germain where, unhappily, the well-loved street market has been forced to close, the Buci feels like another antique shop, full of beautifully chosen and utterly desirable pieces. While their charming, energetic son manages the hotel, the owners love looking for old things, whence a personal *salon* where every picture is worth a good look – the themes are horses and women – and every chair or lamp has a story. In the evening, the morning's gentle classical music turns to jazz to fit the 1930s atmosphere and in the basement piano bar/breakfast space, you can sit on three superbly ornate red sofas and admire yet more pictures and objects. Bedrooms are less unusual but still high class. Done with good repro furniture and remarkable-quality fabrics from top design houses (a different one for each floor), they are yellow and red, blue and cream, checks, stripes and florals in a rich coordination of canopies, pelmets and quilts. The pretty bathrooms are excellent too and you will enjoy the monogrammed linen. A good, reliable and quiet place to stay. *Internet access. English and Spanish spoken.*

rooms	24: 12 doubles, 8 twins, 4 suites.
price	€240–€335, suites €350–€550.
meals	Breakfast €14–€20; afternoon tea served.
metro	St Germain des Prés (4), Mabillon (10).
RER	St Michel-Notre Dame.
buses	39 63 86 87 96
car park	St Germain des Prés.

In the 1500s, the Buci's cellars were Queen Margot's stables. Briefly wife of King Henri IV and a poet, she attracted the great and the good to her brilliant court until the wars of religion burst the country apart.

Frédéric Lassalle

tel	(0)1 55 42 74 74
fax	(0)1 55 42 74 44
e-mail	hotelbuci@wanadoo.fr
web	www.hotelbuci.fr

Hôtel Saint André des Arts
66 rue Saint André des Arts, 75006 Paris

This relaxed, low-cost hotel beside the bustling St André crossroads has been known and loved by backpackers and intellectuals for years. You are met by a row of old choir stalls, a listed staircase and Henri, a former philosophy teacher who is happy to talk *philo* and Proust with you but not the latest in design. White paint sets off the old timbers, new carpets are being laid, new little tiled shower rooms being fitted, windows have been double-glazed – but nothing can ever hide how the old building twists and turns. Some rooms are very small, one is reached across an interior balcony. Some have immensely high ceilings and great windows, beams, old stone walls, 16th-century style. Practical Rustic French Antique furniture is set in a simple, pleasant décor. Breakfast by reception is at a wonderful great 'folding' table set on a *trompe-l'œil* black and white floor that was laid 200 years ago. The neighbourhood is lively, the music sometimes noisy and nocturnal, the atmosphere stimulating. If you feel you would like to join in, don't expect luxury but book early – it's often full. *English, German, Italian, Polish, Spanish spoken.*

rooms	31: 11 doubles, 15 twins/triples, 5 singles.
price	€77–€105.
meals	Breakfast included.
metro	Odéon (4, 10).
RER	St Michel-Notre Dame.
buses	63 70 86 87 96
car park	Rue Mazarine.

Henri & Odile Le Goubin

tel	(0)1 43 26 96 16
fax	(0)1 43 29 73 34
e-mail	hsaintand@minitel.net

Arts really means arts (bows, as in arrows): this was the arms merchants' district. Two muskets discovered under plaster on the old hotel wall betray the origins of the old house.

map 4   entry 55

Hôtel d'Aubusson

33 rue Dauphine, 75006 Paris

Go through the superb old doors into the flagstoned hall – touch the space, hear the quiet piano in the bar, see the promise of moulded, fountained magnificence through the patio doors – and relax. It is an absolutely beautiful stone building, serene and elegant in its golden 17th-century proportions, properly modern in its renovation. Reading by the great hearth in the antique furnished salon or breakfasting in the Aubusson-hung room beyond, you are cocooned in pure French style: a forest of beams high above your head, tall slim windows, superb parquet floors, monogrammed china. There are two lovely patios for summer drinks, the luxurious bar, a Louis XV internet point in a quiet corner. Bedrooms are big or very big (pictured: a superior apartment), some with wonderful beams, all richly, unfussily furnished in custom-made Directoire-style mahogany, thick quiet fabrics, white-and grey-tiled bathrooms (not huge but with all requisites). A grand house where guests are nurtured by classily friendly staff, quietness is a supreme virtue and the ISO Quality Label for service is proudly displayed. *Internet access. English and Spanish spoken.*

The hotel's logo is the coat of arms of the town of Aubusson ('he/she blooms among thorns') where a Royal Tapestry Factory, renowned for its foliage themes, flourished in the 17th century.

rooms	49: 25 doubles, 21 twins, 3 duplex lofts.
price	€260–€340, duplex €410.
meals	Buffet breakfast €20; light meals at hotel's Café Laurent €39, inc. wine + à la carte.
metro	Odéon (4, 10).
RER	St Michel–Notre Dame.
buses	56 63 70 86 87 96
car park	At hotel.

Pascal Gimel

tel	(0)1 43 29 43 43
fax	(0)1 43 29 12 62
e-mail	reservationmichael@hoteldaubusson.com
web	www.hoteldaubusson.com

Hôtel de Nesle
7 rue de Nesle, 75006 Paris

Backpackers' hostel *extraordinaire*, this is **not** a place for clean towels daily, great storage and all quiet by 10.30 pm. But there is none other like it and no other owner like Madame Renée, the lovable matron who, with son David, rules her visitors with voice, gesture and *bonhomie*. The *salon's* old furniture, ancient Larousse and dried flowers give it a carefree atmosphere. And on the first floor is the amazing garden, with roses, apricot trees and pond – half the rooms give onto it. Many rooms carry David's bright frescoes of colonial France: *Afrique* for French explorers and mosquito-netted bed, *Sahara* for private patio and hammam, *Mélanie* for old photographs and lace. All individually furnished with *brocante* and pretty mirrors, soft modern colours and great charm, rooms are spotlessly clean with good mattresses. **But** be careful, even if the price suits and the old beams please, facilities may be too scant for your comfort: virtually no storage, one shower (superb in green marble with romantic broken column) for 10 rooms. *Telephone bookings only (once to book, again to confirm), sharing possible. English spoken.*

rooms	20 doubles: 10 with shower & wc; 10 sharing.
price	€ 60–€ 100.
meals	Available locally.
metro	Odéon (4, 10).
RER	St Michel-Notre Dame.
buses	58 63 70 86 87 96
car park	Rue Mazarine.

Madame Busillet & David Busillet

tel	(0)1 43 54 62 41
fax	(0)1 43 54 31 88
e-mail	contact@hoteldenesle.com
web	www.hoteldenesle.com

The Tower of Nesle was (in)famous for housing princesses who seduced and 'used' handsome young men then threw them into the river to conceal the evidence of their depravities.

map 4   entry 57

Hôtel de Seine

52 rue de Seine, 75006 Paris

Underneath the arches, through the big doors: it still feels like a private mansion and the delightful welcome adds to this impression. There are two really French *salons* off the hall, fresh flowers, space, deep quiet. The breakfast room, presided over by a fine little Pan, aims to please all sorts with a large table for the sociable and several small tables for the less so; walls are clothed in Florentine-style fabric, chairs are blue and studded, antique corner cupboards glow, swags and tassles bobble but it's not cluttered. Bedrooms have class too, with their strong colour schemes, furniture that is gently painted Louis XVI or highly polished, cane seated Directoire and, again, that sense of being in a home not an anonymous hotel. One room displays rather daring black paint and gilt edging in honour of the 1850s craze for all things Far Eastern; others have quirky layouts dictated by the old architecture. Elegant marble bathrooms are much mirrored and the higher floors naturally carry 18th-century timbers and the occasional balcony for rooftop views or birds-eye vistas of fine Parisian façades. A good place to stay. *English spoken.*

rooms	29: 12 doubles, 9 twins, 5 singles, 3 triples.
price	€ 135-€ 195.
meals	Breakfast € 10-€ 12.
metro	St Germain des Prés (4), Mabillon (10), Odéon (4, 10).
RER	St Michel-Notre Dame.
buses	39 48 58 63 70 86 87 95
car park	Mazarine.

Francis Ford Coppola used to have reels of film delivered openly to the Crillon (Paris's most exclusive palace hotel) while he stayed incognito at the somewhat simpler Seine.

Monsieur Henneveux, Perrine Burel

tel	(0)1 46 34 22 80
fax	(0)1 46 34 04 74
e-mail	hotel-de-seine@wanadoo.fr
web	www.hotel-de-seine.com

Welcome Hôtel

66 rue de Seine, 75006 Paris

On one of the trendiest crossroads of Paris where the delightfully twisty, fashionable little un-cheap shopping streets and the legendary cafés of St Germain meet, the Welcome has that comfortable atmosphere created by a natural and unpretentious attitude to life and people. The ground-floor reception is tiny but there's a bit more space as you move up. On the first floor is the small, timbered, tapestried, Louis XIII *salon* whence you can look down from the breakfast table onto the bustle below. Most of the bedrooms are smallish, too, and all give onto one or other of the streets, so you will be grateful for efficient double glazing. Among all sorts of angles and juttings-out, the variegated décor has been attractively revivified with bright new fabrics, gentle wallpapers and smart bottle-green carpeting; furniture is well-designed, functional wood, and bathrooms are prettily tiled. On the top floor you find sloping ceilings and beams: one bedroom is reached through its half-timbered bathroom! It's quirky, probably noisy for the very sensitive, but absolutely in the thick of things. *English and Spanish spoken.*

rooms	30: 17 doubles, 9 twins, 4 singles.
price	€70-€140.
meals	Breakfast €8.
metro	St Germain des Prés (4), Mabillon (10), Odéon (4, 10).
RER	St Michel-Notre Dame.
buses	39 48 58 63 70 86 87 95
car park	St Germain des Prés, St Sulpice.

Monsieur Henneveux, Perrine Burel	
tel	(0)1 46 34 24 80
fax	(0)1 40 46 81 59
web	www.welcomehotel-paris.com

On the corner of Rue de Seine and Rue de Buci is a café with delightfully relaxed young staff who serve coffee as it was done 'in the old days': with vanilla - and a smile.

map 4   entry 59

Millésime Hôtel
15 rue Jacob, 75006 Paris

"Our room had an impossible peacefulness, all I could hear was constant birdsong" a reader says. Behind its imposing old doors, the Millésime is intimate, pretty and quiet – and there cannot be a friendlier, warmer welcome in the whole of St Germain. The colour mix is warmly Mediterranean, with its brick-red and soft ochre sponging all over the lobby, the deep sofas set on glowing parquet and the charming little ochre patio with its climbing plants and tables – three rooms open from the patio itself. This is a fine old building and the new owners have restored the 17th-century staircase with proper respect, despite the lift: it's worth a visit. Bedrooms vary in size but are never too cramped, have pale yellow walls and good white and grey bathrooms. A variety of ancient-looking cast-iron lamps contrast with pretty, contemporary checks and stripes; unusual wood-backed pictures of formal gardens hang on walls, original cord-crossed quilts grace beds; two top-floor rooms have brilliant high-peaked ceilings and roof windows over historic towers and domes. Altogether eminently attractive. *Internet access. English spoken.*

At the end of Rue de Seine, just before the archway to the river, is a quiet little garden dedicated to Champollion, decipherer of the Egyptian hieroglyphs and therefore a national hero.

rooms	22: 16 doubles, 5 twins, 1 single.
price	€ 150–€ 210.
meals	Continental breakfast in room € 12; buffet breakfast € 15.
metro	St Germain des Prés (4).
RER	St Michel-Notre Dame.
buses	39 48 63 86 95
car park	St Germain des Prés.

Marie-Jo Pascassiot

tel	(0)1 44 07 97 97
fax	(0)1 46 34 55 97
e-mail	reservation@millesimehotel.com
web	www.millesimehotel.com

Hôtel des Marronniers

21 rue Jacob, 75006 Paris

Another of the Henneveux private mansion hotels, it stands enviably between quiet courtyard and real garden. The almost dramatically Second Empire *salon*, all ruches and gilt, leads to a delectable old-style conservatory where red-cushioned iron chairs and marble-topped tables wait for you under the fruity 'chandeliers', reflecting the green and shrubby garden – privilege indeed. Room sizes vary: mostly smallish, they all give onto the garden or the front courtyard so no need for double glazing. From the top floor you see higgledy-piggledy rooftops or the church tower, from all rooms you hear the chimes. The décor is based on coordinated fabrics (walls, curtains, canopies, beds), bright floral prints or Regency stripes serving as backdrop to an antique desk, a carved *armoire* or a pair of lemon-tree spray lights. Lots of character here. Recently-renovated bathrooms are most attractive, be they grey and ginger marble or white tiles with an original tropical island 'picture'. After so much light, the basement breakfast room is in soft, dark contrast for cool winter mornings. Or hie ye to the conservatory. *English and Spanish spoken.*

rooms	37: 24 doubles, 8 twins, 3 singles, 2 quadruples.
price	€ 110–€ 245.
meals	Breakfast € 10–€ 12.
metro	St Germain des Prés (4).
RER	St Michel-Notre Dame.
buses	39 48 63 86 95
car park	St Germain des Prés.

Monsieur Henneveux, Perrine Burel	
tel	(0)1 43 25 30 60
fax	(0)1 40 46 83 56
web	www.hotel-marronniers.com

In the courtyard, observe the ineffably Parisian concierge's lodge on the left with its potted plants and lacey curtains and know that you see a dying species: people are being replaced by coded locks and interphones.

map 4   entry 61

Hôtel des Deux Continents
25 rue Jacob, 75006 Paris

The Deux Continents and its three ancient listed buildings sink discreetly into the background among the decorators and antique shops. Its public rooms are hugely atmospheric with beams, gilt frames, draperies and dark furniture, lightened at the front by the big street window and at the back by a little patio. Venus stands shyly among the greenery and tables are laid with fine white cloths and bright china against a green and gold backdrop. The geography is intriguing: two buildings look onto quiet inner courtyards, the larger, noisier rooms are at the front. Some rooms have rooftop views, some look onto flowered terraces, all are done in contemporary-classic style with yards of fabric – walls, bedheads, covers, curtains, pelmets, the odd canopy – in occasionally surprising mixtures of colours and patterns; but it all 'works', as do the bronze lights and pretty old mirrors. In the last building (two storeys, no lift), the smallest rooms are utterly quiet, equally charming and air-conditioned. The whole place has masses of personality, the staff are young and welcoming and St Germain des Prés hums. *English and Italian spoken.*

rooms	41: 27 doubles, 10 twins, 4 triples.
price	€ 135–€ 190.
meals	Breakfast € 10–€ 12.
metro	St Germain des Prés (4).
RER	St Michel-Notre Dame.
buses	39 48 63 86 95
car park	St Germain des Prés.

Which two continents? The Old World and the New. In 1783 America and Great Britain signed the Treaty of Independence in a house just a few blocks down from here.

Monsieur Henneveux, Perrine Burel

tel	(0)1 43 26 72 46
fax	(0)1 43 25 67 80
e-mail	continents.hotel@wanadoo.fr
web	www.2continents-hotel.com

La Villa

29 rue Jacob, 75006 Paris

Soberly studied forms and colours: big blocky black desk, curvy steel stair rail, soft sleek grey silk curtains, big ochre-flecked stone floor slabs; gentle jazz; a series of deep chairs in grey, brown and beige plush on a teak floor by the bar and a smiling ever-present barman (or so it seemed) – this is utterly St Germain des Prés. Staff are appropriately young, bright and attentive, as is Jean-Philippe Nuel's renewed décor. In the bedrooms, the drama of colour is red, black and white, the gentleness is ivory, rich beige, moss green and Regency fashion plates. Materials are rich and yielding – thick blue or wine red curtains folded back on their fine silk linings, 'crocodile' skin bedheads in black wooden frames, fluffy white duvets with dark grey and ivory woollen squares on top, all against a pair of scarlet walls. And the details: monogrammed linen, superb designer bathrooms in chrome and ground glass, big stone-framed mirrors. Breakfast is down the 1930s-look stairs in another stylish place of red, rich skin and engravings. It all feels really good and the bar still attracts a few glitterati in the evenings. *English spoken.*

rooms	31: 23 doubles, 4 twins, 4 junior suites.
price	€195–€350, suites €380–€440.
meals	Breakfast €14; lunch & dinner on request €15–€30.
metro	St Germain des Prés (4).
RER	St Michel–Notre Dame.
buses	39 48 63 86 95
car park	St Germain des Prés.

Christine Horbette

tel	(0)1 43 26 60 00
fax	(0)1 46 34 63 63
e-mail	hotel@villa-saintgermain.com
web	villa-saintgermain.com

On the outside, Rue Jacob is nothing but hotels, interior designers and antique merchants. But push a solid oak door or two and you may find a hidden garden and the gift of peace.

map 4   entry 63

Hôtel du Danube
58 rue Jacob, 75006 Paris

Built in the 1870s as a private mansion, this soft civilised hotel rejoices in a dazzling black and red *salon* and a pale salmon patio where potted palms sit on bright green 'grass', iron tables can be laid for breakfast and elegant façades rise skywards. The quietest rooms look over this or the smaller lightwell with its pretty *trompe-l'œil* skyscape. Others have more activity – and more noise – under their double-glazed windows (the higher, the quieter). Style and fittings vary widely, twisty corridors change levels, it's a warm, long-lived-in place. Superb 'superior' rooms have two windows, some very desirable antiques, armchairs and thick smart fabrics, yet they feel intimate and friendly. Their bathrooms are carefully done too. 'Standard' rooms all have the same blue-laminate bamboo-trim desk units and nice 'wooden-plank' wallpaper with some quaintly old-style bathroom tiling – but all necessities are there. The attic room is the most appealing of these. And you all meet as equals in the charming countrified breakfast room and appreciate the bevy of young helpful staff at reception. *Internet access. English and Spanish spoken.*

Surprising that so glorious a figure as Napoleon should have such a small street for his surname - maybe they couldn't quite forget the two million who died fighting his battles.

rooms	41: 25 doubles, 10 twins, 5 family rooms, 1 junior suite.
price	€120–€160, family rooms & suite €210.
meals	Breakfast €9.
metro	St Germain des Prés (4).
RER	Musée d'Orsay.
buses	39 48 63 95 96
car park	St Germain des Prés.

Séverin Ferrand & Michel Sario

tel	(0)1 42 60 34 70
fax	(0)1 42 60 81 18
e-mail	info@hoteldanube.fr
web	www.hoteldanube.fr

L'Hôtel

13 rue des Beaux Arts, 75006 Paris

The hotel. Step inside, look down a rich tunnel of gildings, marble and plush, through the deep-stuccoed *Bélier* restaurant (seriously good food from a fine young chef) to the light in the patio where the old fountain sings; stand on the inlaid star, look up, up, up the inimitable atrium, past pilasters and galleries to... more light – intimations of infinity? Fabulously renovated by Jacques Garcia into outrageous opulence with due respect for music-hall star Mistinguett: her all-mirrors Art Deco bedroom brilliantly reset in crushed velvet, and Oscar Wilde: he died a pauper here and wouldn't know 'his' room, a crimson and mahogany marvel – with terrace. *Le Cardinal* has, naturally, the biggest, luxiest gold and scarlet suite – with terrace. *Charles X* is softly restful in pale gold Regency stripes with a touch of purple. All rooms are strikingly different, some a lot smaller but huge in character. Bathrooms, some gasp-worthy, have rich marble alcoves. Charming staff and a mass of genuine antiques, pictures and *objets*, make this a place for connoisseurs of taste and comfort. Go on – splurge. *English, Finnish, Italian, Japanese spoken*

rooms	20: 14 double/twins, 2 twins, 3 junior suites, 1 apartment for 4.
price	€ 248–€529; suite €529–€625; apartment €625–€721.
meals	Buffet breakfast €16.80. Set lunchmenu €24.50; lunch or dinner à la carte €35–€50.
metro	St Germain des Prés.
RER	St Michel-Notre Dame, Châtelet-Les Halles.
buses	39 48 95

Fabienne Capelli & Béatrice Ruggieri

tel	(0)1 44 41 99 00
fax	(0)1 43 25 64 81
e-mail	reservation@l-hotel.com
web	l-hotel.com

Ever the poet, Jorge Luis Borgès, urgently awaited by Mitterand for his Legion of Honour, offered to autograph books for guests. "But you're late for the President, Mr Borgès!" "Oh, one's always late for someone."

map 4   entry 65

Hôtel de Lille
40 rue de Lille, 75007 Paris

Fun-lovers? Gather in the cafés of St Germain des Prés. Culture fans? Swan off to Orsay. Between the two you sleep at this small, simple, cleancut hotel, a bargain among the smart antique shops. The strict 1930s style of the lobby is softened by big packets of greenery at the window and another universe looms downstairs: the stone vault makes the breakfast space feel old, soft-padded wicker furniture makes it tempting. Bedrooms are to scale: small, compact, furnished with 1930s veneered or cane and bamboo pieces; white walls and red carpets are a good foil to lively coordinated prints of curtain, quilt and stools; top-floor rooms are even cosier with their beams. In a flash of humour, one room is all done in Jouy fabric depicting a collection of Chinamen in a hot-air balloon; bathrooms are newly renovated in smart white-grey friezed tiles, good little ginger 'granite' basins and big mirrors. Staff and owner are friendly and relaxed and he keeps an eagle eye on the state of your quilt. Refurbishment is constant, hair dryers are in place, the bar is most attractive. *English and Portuguese spoken. Internet access.*

You may remember the Lille from your student days when washing facilities were communal, the price was 30 francs per night and the walls were made of cork!

rooms	20: 9 doubles, 6 twins, 5 singles.
price	€93–€142.
meals	Breakfast included.
metro	Rue du Bac (12), St Germain des Prés (4), Tuileries (1).
RER	Musée d'Orsay.
buses	8 49 68 69 95
car park	Montalembert.

Michel Margouilla
tel	(0)1 42 61 29 09
fax	(0)1 42 61 53 97
e-mail	hotel-de-lille@wanadoo.fr
web	www.hotel-paris-lille.com

Hôtel du Quai Voltaire

19 quai Voltaire, 75007 Paris

Pissarro's painting of quintessential Paris-on-Seine was done here and only four rooms do not see 'his' view. Baudelaire also stayed here, as did Wagner, Sibelius and Françoise Sagan: the Voltaire was something of an institution and still feels like a well-loved club with its rather worn, golden-fringed armchairs in the panelled *salon* and its guests who come back again and again, some for over 30 years. Lively, humorous and enthusiastic, Régine Lepeinteur loves the contact with guests, old and new, and keeps the artistic tradition going: she shows the works of young painters and sculptors, displays jewellery samples in a glass cabinet, keeps the breakfast room like an old-time bistro. Rooms are small, beds are standard French 140cm wide, some baths are not for reclining, but mattresses are good, staff are superb old retainers and the welcoming atmosphere is warmly genuine. New bathroom fixtures should be coming soon. A warning, however: you will need earplugs as the price of that view is no protection against traffic noise. Three top-floor singles with bathroom on floor below at bargain prices. English and German spoken.

rooms	33: 17 doubles, 9 twins, 6 singles, 1 triple.
price	€ 102–€ 150.
meals	Breakfast € 8.
metro	Rue du Bac (12), Tuileries (1).
RER	Musée d'Orsay.
buses	24 27 39 48 68 73 95
car park	Musée d'Orsay.

Régine Lepeinteur

tel	(0)1 42 61 50 91
fax	(0)1 42 61 62 26
e-mail	info@quaivoltaire.fr
web	www.quaivoltaire.fr

Pissarro's magical shimmering vision of the Seine, the Pont Royal, the Louvre and the trees along the embankment can be seen at the Musée d'Orsay just down the road; the others are in Russia.

map 4   entry 67

Hôtel Verneuil

8 rue de Verneuil, 75007 Paris

The welcoming *salon* is like a real drawing room: bits and pieces of family history, tempting books, chairs to curl up in. Your small bedroom – they are all different and some only just make three-star size – may have painted beams, a carved bedhead, a canopy, neo-classical pilasters, some of Sylvie de Lattre's fascinating and carefully-chosen collection of engravings, portraits and drawings. The décor is one of understated strength, bedcovers are thick white piqué, walls are dressed in fine fabrics or plain pastels to set off special features. Beds are firm, all bedding was renewed in 2002 and windows are hung with fine linen nets as well as beautiful coordinated curtains. One 'standard' double room, reached by walking under a massive old beam, is like a little red box, warm and intimate. Bathrooms are small but complete and the vaulted basement breakfast room has an easy rustic air. Your hostess and her staff will make you feel as at home as in a private house and this quietly classy hotel is a delicious find among the antique shops and galleries of Saint Germain. *English, German, Italian and Spanish spoken.*

The Duke of Verneuil's Marchioness mother got the title, plus a small fortune, from King Henri IV, father of her illegitimate son, but never the crown he'd promised.

rooms	26: 17 doubles, 4 twins, 5 singles.
price	€120–€185.
meals	Continental buffet breakfast €12.
metro	St Germain des Prés (4), Rue du Bac (12).
RER	Musée d'Orsay, St Michel-Notre Dame.
buses	39 48 68 69 73 95
car park	St Germain des Prés.

Sylvie de Lattre & Sandrine Troccaz

tel	(0)1 42 60 82 14
fax	(0)1 42 61 40 38
e-mail	hotelverneuil@wanadoo.fr
web	www.hotelverneuil.com

Hôtel de l'Université
22 rue de l'Université, 75007 Paris

The old entrance, the vista through to bits of greenery, the split-level timber-framed *salon*, the wide stairs leading easily to high-ceilinged bedrooms are all privileges in a city where a square metre is worth a lingot – even the smaller rooms are pretty, with neat little bathrooms. The Université is like a grand embracing home with antiques and *objets* that Madame Bergmann has discovered far and wide over the years: tapestries in the right places, old prints in old frames ("Authentic or nothing – don't hold with copies", she says), carvings, lamps. For breakfast by the tiny patio there's a long black velvet bench at a long marble bistro table (or under the honeysuckle if you're in one of the stunning terrace rooms). Most rooms have writing table or armchair or sofa and peaceful colours to set them off, some have original panelling. Bathrooms are good – lots of marble, the right accessories; so are views – neo-classical ministry portico, the École Nationale d'Administration, cradle of many a great career. The Université is a determinedly old-fashioned, eminently civilised delight for the discerning. *English, German, Italian spoken.*

rooms	27: 8 doubles, 9 twins, 10 singles.
price	€110–€200.
meals	Continental-plus breakfast €9; lunch & dinner on request €15–€30.
metro	St Germain des Prés (4).
RER	Musée d'Orsay.
buses	24 27 39 48 63 68 69 70 87 95
car park	Montalembert.

Madame Bergmann & Monsieur Teissedre	
tel	(0)1 42 61 09 39
fax	(0)1 42 60 40 84
e-mail	hoteluniversite@wanadoo.fr
web	www.hoteluniversite.com

In the 12th century, the monks of St Germain Abbey used to have their ice house in the powerfully vaulted basement of this hotel, where there is now a superb sitting room for guests.

map 4   entry 69

Hôtel Lenox Saint Germain

9 rue de l'Université, 75007 Paris

The lobby is a serious symphony of pure 1930s style: strict lines, straight and curved, plain natural materials, a fascinating frieze motif and a superb framed inlay of a panther. Some great bronze animals too. The friendly staff will make you feel immediately welcome. Through the arch, the Lenox Bar has tremendous atmosphere with its inlaid jazzmen all over the walls. Used by the Gallimard publishing team for drinks after work, by film stars for interviews, by writers for long literary arguments, it is utterly St Germain des Prés. But breakfast is now in the vaulted wraparound Nile-scene basement. Upstairs, there are big rooms and (much) smaller ones, all different. Some have old furniture, some have modern synthetic units, hand-painted cupboards, intriguing 1930s pieces. Colour schemes are mostly muted. Rooms on the little side street are quieter than the others, corner rooms with two windows and lots of light are super, or you may have the luxury of a balcony. Bathrooms are good and extra shelving for pots and paints is provided by little trolleys. An excellent place for feeling you belong in St Germain. *English, German, Italian, Spanish spoken.*

The tramp hero of Les Amants du Pont Neuf spent a month in the Best Room here while filming but was forbidden to wash for the sake of more authentic tramphood. Pity.

rooms	34: 17 doubles, 12 twins, 5 junior suites for 2.
price	€ 142–€ 150, suites € 185–€ 270.
meals	Breakfast € 10–€ 12.50; Lenox Club snacks € 5–€ 10.
metro	St Germain des Prés (4).
RER	Musée d'Orsay.
buses	48 39 63 68 69 83 94
car park	Rue des Saints Pères.

Madame Laporte & Mademoiselle Colson

tel	(0)1 42 96 10 95
fax	(0)1 42 61 52 83
e-mail	hotel@lenoxsaintgermain.com
web	www.lenoxsaintgermain.com

Hôtel de l' Académie

32 rue des Saints Pères, 75007 Paris

Leave a street bustling with motor traffic and beautiful people for a quiet haven. Generally relaxed staff (Parisians can be easily stressed) may beckon you towards the depths, past the humour of a brilliantly *trompe-l'œil* dreamscape of classical damsels and exotic birds, to a big *salon* furnished essentially in Second Empire style – gildings and furbelows, tassels and bronze bits – beneath a splendid glass canopy. In the bedrooms, and with contemporary expectations in mind, bathrooms are fully equipped, bedding is new, plain-painted walls are a foil for old beams and choice pieces such as a nice old ormulu Louis XV chest with its elaborate trim. A couple of little kidney-shaped bedside tables are charmers. Some rooms are more daringly done in rococo and crimson damask. The basement breakfast room starts with papyrus pictures from the land of the pyramids then flips between the style inspired by Napoleon's Egyptian campaign and an elaborate Hispanic-carving mode. You can have a caterer dinner here too if you wish. Bedrooms are biggish, by Paris standards, and storage space has been carefully planned. *English, German, Spanish spoken.*

rooms	35: 20 doubles, 10 twins, 5 junior suites.
price	€99–€229, suites €199–€299.
meals	Full buffet breakfast €14.50; lunch & dinner on request c€25
metro	St Germain des Prés (4).
RER	Musée d'Orsay.
buses	48 63 86 95
car park	Consult hotel.

The 'Holy Fathers' were not monks of the Abbey of St Germain: the name is a deformation of St Pierre, an old parish church that is now the Ukrainian Catholic St Vladimir.

Gérard & Katia Chekroun

tel	(0)1 45 49 80 00
fax	(0)1 45 44 75 24
e-mail	academiehotel@aol.com
web	www.academiehotel.com

map 4   entry 71

Le Madison

143 boulevard Saint Germain, 75006 Paris

Discreet behind a row of trees opposite the vastly celebrated *Deux Magots* café, the Madison's fine Art Deco façade is as supremely Parisian as its antique-filled *salons*. The enlightened owner likes sharing his collections: a fine portrait of his mother as a young girl dominates the velour-clothed breakfast tables while a powerful porcelain cockerel crows from its pedestal. This is a very stylish city hotel with top-quality fabrics and fittings, yet it's like no other: Maryse Burkard's adventurous imagination guides the rich choice of colours and textures, bathrooms have stunning Italian tiling, lift doors carry wonderful artists' impressions of the great names of St Germain and staff have just the right mix of polite class and friendly cheerfulness. All rooms are different, bursting with personality. In a big blue, beige and green room over the boulevard: a lovely green china lamp on a nice old desk and a deep red marble bathroom; next door, a small raspberry, yellow and royal blue room, vital and provocative; in the top-floor suite, a triumph of space and wraparound views. If it's full, try the Bourgogne & Montana. *English, Portuguese and Spanish spoken.*

In an earlier life, the Madison was a simple place of rest for thin purses: Camus stayed here when writing L'Etranger. Now big-name fashion boutiques draw the fatter wallets.

rooms	54: 27 doubles, 19 twins, 7 singles, 1 suite for 4.
price	€ 140–€ 290; suite € 290–€ 380.
meals	Breakfast included; lunch & dinner on request € 15–€ 30.
metro	St Germain des Prés (4).
RER	Châtelet-Les Halles.
buses	48 58 63 70 86 87 95 96
car park	St Germain des Prés; St Sulpice.

Maryse Burkard

tel	(0)1 40 51 60 00
fax	(0)1 40 51 60 01
e-mail	resa@hotel-madison.com
web	www.hotel-madison.com

Hôtel Bourgogne et Montana

3 rue de Bourgogne, 75007 Paris

Luxury of the four-star variety has now taken over the whole of this marvellous hotel where the quiet, sober atmosphere may possibly reflect the serious work being done in the nearby National Assembly – or not – but does not prohibit the delightful, efficient staff from taking a light hearted, friendly attitude. The owner's grandfather, a bored MP in the 1890s, drew those wicked caricatures of his solemn colleagues; his own antiques and pictures are placed for your pleasure in the famous raspberry rotunda, the primrose *salon* and the deeply tempting breakfast room that is full of light and the most sinful buffet (included in the price). This combination of wit and creature comforts is peculiarly French and civilised. So abandon yourself to the caress of fine damask and deep velvet, smart contemporary designer fabrics and oh-so-French traditional Jouy prints. The bigger rooms and suites have space and antiques, thick quilted upholstery and some extraordinary bathrooms; the smaller ones are like rich, embracing nests. If it's full, try the Madison. *Pets €13. English and Spanish spoken.*

rooms	32: 15 doubles, 8 twins, 3 singles, 2 suites for 4, 4 suites for 4.
price	€140–€220; suites €290–€335.
meals	Breakfast buffet included.
metro	Assemblée Nationale (12), Invalides (8).
RER	& Air France bus: Invalides.
buses	93 83 63
car park	Invalides.

Rumour has it that a royal mistress lived here and went secretly to the king via a tunnel to the Louvre. But... the French Revolution of 1789 destroyed the monarchy and this building is dated 1791.

Stéphane Beauvivre

tel	(0)1 45 51 20 22
fax	(0)1 45 56 11 98
e-mail	bourgogne-montana.com

map 1   entry 73

Port du Gros Caillou
Rue Jeanne Hachette
Rue de la Comète
Rue des Favorites

Big Rock - Joan Littleaxe - Comet - The Favourites

Hôtel de Varenne

44 rue de Bourgogne, 75007 Paris

A new broom is sweeping through this hotel: brand new bedding, a change of carpets and wall fabric in the peachy little breakfast room, fine black metal furniture in the ever-endearing garden courtyard – and more to come. A new owner has to take stock and plan his renovations over time, as we know you will understand – the Varenne will not transform in a day but opposite the sleek new front door, the intimidatingly high reception desk has given way to a friendly old writing table. There's a country air to the bedrooms: lots of soft deep pink or beige on walls and floors, plus greens and creams and coffee colours in curtains and friezes. Half of them in Louis XVI style (that beige and a soft peach pink), half Empire (in stronger tones), no two rooms are alike, most are a reasonable size and all have one or two really nice old pieces of furniture; there are plush-covered bucket armchairs, attractive framed prints and well-kept bathrooms, 13 of them retiled and fitted. The four rooms that give onto the street are noisier but bigger. The charming staff are constantly on the lookout for more they can do to make your stay special. *English and German spoken.*

rooms	27: 14 doubles, 10 twins, 3 triples.
price	€ 115–€ 147.
meals	Breakfast € 9.
metro	Varenne (13), Invalides (8, 13).
RER	& Air France bus: Invalides.
buses	69
car park	Invalides.

Jean-Marc Pommier

tel	(0)1 45 51 45 55
fax	(0)1 45 51 86 63
e-mail	info@hoteldevarenne.com
web	www.hoteldevarenne.com

In old French, 'varenne' meant uncultivated, game-rich land. In the 16th century, this area of Paris was the hunting reserve of the Lord of Saint Germain, occasionally joined by the King.

map 1   entry 74

Hôtel du Palais Bourbon

49 rue de Bourgogne, 75007 Paris

Fine old mansions, now occupied by civil servants of course, line the streets and nothing prepares you for an hotel that spreads and rambles like a country house. You will be greeted by the delightful South American Rafael, or Monsieur, or Madame Mère; the atmosphere is comfortably casual and loyal staff stay for years. After the fresh, high-beamed breakfast room and lobby, you enter the depths of several connecting buildings, full of secret spaces. Gentle staircases announce their 18th-century origins; all the rooms are different, those on the lower floors are unusually big for two Parisian stars, top-floor doubles have beamy character, the smallest are due for alteration. The quiet unprovocative décor is based on soft pastels in peachy paint or mild stripes or delicate florals and each room has an individual touch, be it an oriental rug or a country antique, as well as essential furniture – beds, wardrobes, desk units – that is custom-made in Brittany. Recently-renovated bathrooms are simply excellent with white tiling and pretty friezes, ultra-modern tap fittings, generous space. Altogether remarkable value. *English and Spanish spoken.*

The 'Bourbon Palace' was seized from its aristocratic owners in 1790 to become the 'House of the Revolution': the National Assembly has sat there since the Restoration.

rooms	30: 15 doubles, 5 twins, 10 triple/quadruples.
price	€ 61–€ 155 including breakfast.
meals	Breakfast included.
metro	Invalides (8), Varenne (8), Assemblée Nationale (12).
RER	Invalides.
buses	24 63 69 73 83 84 94
car park	Invalides.

Thierry Claudon

tel	(0)1 44 11 30 70
fax	(0)1 45 55 20 21
e-mail	htlbourbon@aol.com
web	www.hotel-palais-bourbon.com

Hôtel Latour Maubourg

150 rue de Grenelle, 75007 Paris

If you think the outside looks like a friendly old house, you'll know you are right once you step inside to be greeted by a smiling owner and Faust the eager spaniobeagle. You may borrow cutlery and have your evening picnic in the comfortable panelled and family-furnished sitting/dining room where good armchairs occupy a couple of corners by the great brown marble fireplace, good books await your curiosity and tall veranda windows bring light from the patio. Bedrooms, in all shapes, sizes and styles, have the same air of smart old guest rooms: the occasional original marble fireplace, old-fashioned engravings, rather dated décor – bucket armchairs, old-style fabrics – and 1970s bathrooms. The ground floor suite is a pair of magnificent rooms, once the mansion's drawing rooms, flooded with light and deeply grand in their huge ancestral portraits of a beturbanned German and his lady, mouldings, chandeliers and fireplaces, and now a good big bathroom. There are so few rooms that you can be sure that charming Madame Orsenne will have plenty of time for you. *Two floors, no lift. Internet access. Laundry service. English and German spoken.*

rooms	10: 5 doubles, 2 twins, 2 singles, 1 suite for 5.
price	€125–€185, suite €215–€305, including breakfast.
meals	Breakfast included; lunch & dinner on request €6–€20.
metro	Latour-Maubourg (8).
RER	& Air France bus: Invalides.
buses	20 20 63 69
car park	Invalides.

Like everyone else near Napoleon's tomb, Latour Maubourg was a military gent who faithfully fought all the Emperor's wars and was then clever enough to become the restored King Louis XVIII's War Minister.

Victor & Maria Orsenne

tel	(0)1 47 05 16 16
fax	(0)1 47 05 16 14
e-mail	info@latour-maubourg.fr
web	www.latour-maubourg.fr

map 3   entry 76

Grand Hôtel Lévêque

29 rue Cler, 75007 Paris

Beneath its fluttering flags, the door to the ever-popular Lévêque hides from this lively, colourful pedestrian street where shops overflow onto pavements. At the end of the long, narrow classic-style hallway is the desk where the kindly, if occasionally busy, receptionist deals patiently with all comers; the constant flow of young travellers makes for an amicable polyglot atmosphere. The little rounded sitting corner with its superb new flooring and red plush bench draws the eye: you may prefer to be with the genuine Parisians outside but do admire Alexandra de Lazareff's fascinating bronze animals here. They are proof, in a way, that the owners respect their guests and want to create a civilised space in this big, bustling house; the sepia mural of Notre Dame is another example of this attitude. Bedroom décor is pretty much the same throughout with fine new bedcovers in yellow and green, 1930s-style laminated bedheads, green carpets, pastel fabrics and sometimes an old mirror-fronted wardrobe – all neat and clean with decent shower rooms, good beds and adequate storage space. *Cold drinks distributor. English and Italian spoken.*

Until the 1830s, when the developers moved in, this area, called Grenelle, was a vast plain owned by a great abbey with just a farm, a small château and a military execution block.

rooms	50: 20 doubles, 20 twins, 5 singles, 5 triples.
price	€ 50–€ 114.
meals	Breakfast € 7.
metro	École Militaire, Latour Maubourg (8).
RER	& Air France bus: Invalides.
buses	28 69 80 92
car park	Latour Maubourg.

Christian Tourneur

tel	(0)1 47 05 49 15
fax	(0)1 45 50 49 36
e-mail	info@hotel-leveque.com
web	www.hotel-leveque.com

Hôtel Amélie

5 rue Amélie, 75007 Paris

So small and sweet and modest with its geranium-hung windowsills onto the village-like street – this is the perfect little unpretentious hotel where you will feel snug and cared for by the young owners. There is no surplus space but the sunnily-clothed front room is a tempting place for a fresh-as-fresh French breakfast and the rest of the house is in keeping. The old wooden stair rail snakes up the four floors where doors the colour of sunripe tomatoes open onto pretty prints and cotton piqué bedcovers in blue and yellow or red and green. Furniture is painted white or laminated grey and yellow. There is light and freshness everywhere, bathrooms are newly tiled and even the neighbours are working for your pleasure. rooms over the courtyard have views of trees and flowerboxes on windowsills opposite. This is a family-run place: they are natural, humorous, relaxed, they treat people as people and clearly enjoy the job. And you will never feel lost in the crowd. Really good, friendly value. *Four floors, no lift. Arabic, English and German spoken.*

rooms	16: 8 doubles, 4 twins, 4 singles.
price	€72–€92.
meals	Breakfast €6.10.
metro	Latour-Maubourg (8), Invalides (8, 13).
RER	Invalides.
buses	28 69 80 92
car park	Garage opposite hotel.

Who was this Amélie, she of the pretty name and quiet little street? No great romantic lady, just the daughter of the landlord who died at 15 "an example of all the Christian virtues".

Michel & Monika Orville

tel	(0)1 45 51 74 75
fax	(0)1 45 56 93 55
e-mail	hotelamelie@wanadoo.fr
web	www.hotelamelie.fr

map 3   entry 78

Hôtel Le Valadon

16 rue Valadon, 75007 Paris

Victor Orsenne has created an original and intelligent formula: the 'modern-design budget hotel'. More guesthouse than hotel, the Valadon is small, functional and very convivial. Beyond the unassuming doorway, the lobby may feel a little stark and hostelly but the ten bedrooms in the main building, identically decorated in black, white, red and beige, have light and great style. Each has a double bed and a single divan: these are real triples with enough space for three. Behind the bed, a dark grey wall relieved by three horizontal red stripes; at the window and wrapping the divan, bold black and white stripes plus red cushions; a white laminated desk, shelf and hanging unit; a silky steel column carrying oval mirror and television. Bathrooms are grey and white with more red stripes. All very striking and attractive. Downstairs, there's a communal refrigerator and guests can share their evening picnics in the dining veranda – six little black tables and square plates loaned by the hotel. Beyond the courtyard, the family room in more traditional pastels enjoys the terrace, a downstairs bathroom and another connecting room. *English spoken. Internet access.*

Improbable as it may sound nowadays, this street was designed by an architect, in 1843, then named after him. History does not tell of his relationship to the government agent who commissioned him.

rooms	12: 11 triples, 1 double.
price	€ 85–€ 140, including breakfast.
meals	Breakfast included.
metro	École Militaire (8).
RER	& Air France bus: Invalides.
buses	28 69 80 87 92
car park	Invalides.

Maria & Victor Orsenne

tel	(0)1 47 53 89 85
fax	(0)1 44 18 90 56
e-mail	info@hotelvaladon.com
web	www.hotelvaladon.com

Hôtel Relais Bosquet-Tour Eiffel

19 rue du Champ de Mars, 75007 Paris

Beyond the big, colourful, cushioned *salon* are two attractive breakfast spaces, one for smokers, one for abstainers – space and peace come with remarkable care for the client's comfort here. Owners and reception staff are quietly attentive; each room has iron and board, kettle, four pillows, modem socket, masses of hangers and electric blackout blinds. Half the extraordinarily attractive rooms are round the courtyard where magnolia and creepers flourish, half look onto the street. The smart contemporary/trad décor, either red, blue or green themed, avoids plushness by its easy use of rich, bright, coordinated fabrics; big upholstered stools make superb luggage racks and fine white bathrooms have just a sober bit of coloured trim. There's space in these rooms and good storage, beds are zippable twin doubles (extra long in 'superior' rooms) and the lighting is just right; every print has been chosen for its character and framed accordingly; the occasional antique is an added personal touch and staff will organise baby sitters or secretarial workers for you. A most likeable hotel two minutes from the Eiffel Tower. *English and Italian spoken*

rooms	40 doubles/twins.
price	€ 125–€ 160.
meals	Generous continental breakfast € 10.50.
metro	Metro: Ecole Militaire (8).
RER	Pont de l'Alma.
buses	28 69 82 80 87 92
car park	Consult hotel.

Dora & Philippe Hervois

tel	(0)1 47 05 25 45
fax	(0)1 45 55 08 24
e-mail	hotel@relaisbosquet.com
web	www.relaisbosquet.com

General Bosquet saved the English army fighting under Lord Cardigan at Inkerman (Crimea) and was made Field Marshal and Senator of France for it on his return to France in 1856.

map 3   entry 80

Hôtel Le Tourville

16 avenue de Tourville, 75007 Paris

Behind its smart Art Deco face, the Tourville is relaxed and not over-luxy despite its four stars. Anyway, the attentive welcome is worth a skyful of stars. A soft, cushioned impression flows from deep carpets with the Turkey rugs that lighten and colour the whole hotel, plush sofas to sink into, indoor shutters that filter the afternoon sun, muted Vivaldi. Sensuous colours and shapes are everywhere – butter yellow, fir green, soft strokable materials, gatepost ornaments on an Empire console: like all the Bouvier/Agaud hotels, it has ironical decorative touches, full of intelligence and fun. Each room has a few 'finds' – a brass-handled chest, a Regency writing table, an old mirror, irony in frames. A big ground-floor room has a terrace and a neo-classical group of nude women; junior suites are generous with space and light – and more kitsch pictures. Colours are peach, salmon or frankly pink; some rooms are small for the category but all have good storage and super bathrooms, with maybe a Victorian clothes horse or an old nursery chair in contrast. Simple sophistication is the style, and very attractive it is too. *English spoken.*

rooms	30: 14 doubles, 13 twins, 3 suites for 4.
price	€ 145–€ 240, suites € 310.
meals	Continental buffet breakfast € 12; lunch & dinner on request € 15–€ 30.
metro	École Militaire (8).
RER	& Air France bus: Invalides.
buses	28 69 80 82 87 92
car park	École Militaire.

Tourville was a romantic admiral called Anne (sic) who fought pirates in the Mediterranean and spent the 1690s locked in endless naval battles with the English in the Channel.

Michel Bouvier & Thierry Jacquet

tel	(0)1 47 05 62 62
fax	(0)1 47 05 43 90
e-mail	hotel@tourville.com
web	www.hoteltourville.com

Hôtel de Londres Eiffel

1 rue Augereau, 75007 Paris

Halfway between the Eiffel Tower (affectionately known as *La Grande Dame*) and the gilded lid over Napoléon's simple place of rest (he was less kindly known as the Little Corporal), here is a friendly, warm-coloured hotel in butter-yellow and raspberry-pink, with friezes and quilting. The mixture of fine blinds and heavy curtains makes for a most welcoming atmosphere in the lobby and round into the sitting/dining area. Here are marble-topped tables, pink-skirted and beribboned chairs and gilt-framed mirrors. Beyond, past a pair of plant-filled lightwells, is the *pavillon* with six bedrooms on two floors in sweet seclusion. All rooms play variations on the same pink and yellow theme with very pretty florals, checks and stripes — even the blankets under the bedcovers are coordinated ochre or red. Gustavian style (Directoire France revisited by Sweden) is to replace the old French furniture. Some bath/shower rooms are attractively new, some a little more old-fashioned but perfectly adequate. But above all, you will be very well looked after by the eager and enthusiastic Madame Prigent. *Free internet access. English spoken.*

rooms	30. 15 doubles, 7 twins, 7 singles, 1 triple.
price	€95–€137.
meals	Breakfast €7.
metro	École Militaire (8).
RER	Pont de l'Alma.
buses	28 69 80 82 87 92
car park	École Militaire.

Isabelle Prigent

tel	(0)1 45 51 63 02
fax	(0)1 47 05 28 96
e-mail	info@londres-eiffel.com
web	www.londres-eiffel.com

Augereau, humble son of a man-servant and a fruit-picker, rose to fame, glory and a whole rollcall of titles under Napoléon: Field Marshal, Duke and Great Eagle of the Legion of Honour.

map 1   entry 82

Hôtel de la Tulipe

33 rue Malar, 75007 Paris

Such a delight, the Tulipe, with its Provençal looks, intelligent atmosphere and civilised owners who are a pleasure to meet. Before the *Exposition Universelle* in 1900 it was a convent. Deliciously intimate rooms are in the former nuns' cells (at least two cells per room!) on two storeys round the cobbled honeysuckled courtyard or over the quiet street. Beams and old stones, yellow-sponged walls, deep red carpets and luminous fabrics, simple pine or wicker furniture: the sun shines here every day of the year. The super, newly-renovated bathrooms have blue, red or yellow country-style tiling and bright butter-yellow paint. Two rooms, one equipped for disabled guests, lead directly off the patio and feel especially peaceful and connected. The breakfast room is charming and sensual with its Burgundy stone floor, blond timbers, interesting paintings... and croissants fresh from the local bakery. Above all, together with the Fortuit family's unpretentious good taste, we remember their smiles and relaxed manner and so, most certainly, will you. *No lift, two floors. Internet café 100m. Wine on sale for private consumption. English, German, Spanish spoken.*

The 7th arrondissement has some stupendous Art Nouveau buildings, many by Jules Lavirotte, a brilliant designer of cement fantasmagorias. Try Avenue Rapp for a taste.

rooms	21: 12 doubles, 5 twins, 3 triples, 1 suite for 4 with 2 bathrooms.
price	€100–€150; suite €220–€240.
meals	Continental breakfast €9.
metro	Invalides (8, 13).
RER	Invalides, Pont de l'Alma.
buses	49 63 69 80 92
car park	Rue Malar.

Caroline & Jean-Louis Fortuit

tel	(0)1 45 51 67 21
fax	(0)1 47 53 96 37
e-mail	hoteldelatulipe@wanadoo.fr
web	www.hoteldelatulipe.com

Rue d'Ankara
Rue Géricault
Square Roland Garros

Ankara - (Théodore) Géricault - Roland Garros

Hôtel Boileau

81 rue Boileau, 75016 Paris

The Boileau is a house of peace, its sweet little face decorated with blue awnings – and only 20 minutes by train from Versailles. Ideal for tennis at Roland Garros or rugby at the Parc des Princes, too. The atmosphere encouraged by the new young owner is easy and welcoming yet attentively efficient. There's a collection of old sewing machines and cash registers to delight lovers of early mechanical devices; mirrors, furniture and pictures from Brittany and Morocco to please the traveller; a fresh green patio, to bring light and air to the southern-style breakfast room at the centre of the three low buildings. Rooms are simply delightful, nothing posh, nothing superfluous, just good warm colour schemes, some original painted Breton bedheads, some lamps in Arab filigree work, interesting pictures and good, pretty bathrooms. Even the little singles have been given the personal touch. Breakfast (a good spread) is served by friendly, entertaining staff who have been here for years. Excellent value, a perfect spot for those going to or from Normandy or Brittany – and such nice people. *English, German and Spanish spoken. Three storeys, no lift.*

No. 86 rue Boileau leads to Villa Mulhouse, 67 little houses built new and modern for his workers in 1835 by cotton magnate Dollfus who believed that hygiene and morality go hand in hand.

rooms	30: 16 doubles, 4 twins, 7 singles, 3 triples.
price	€ 69–€ 110.
meals	Continental-plus breakfast € 7.
metro	Exelmans (9).
RER	& Air France bus: Charles de Gaulle-Étoile; Javel.
buses	22 62 72 PC
car park	Avenue de Versailles.

Fabrice Royer

tel	(0)1 42 88 83 74
fax	(0)1 45 27 62 98
e-mail	boileau@noos.fr
web	www.hotel-boileau.com

Hôtel Trocadéro-La Tour

5 bis rue Massenet, 75116 Paris

Under the new owner, the panelled and mirrored ground floor of the former Hôtel Massenet still has the atmosphere of a quiet old club with its highly polished floor, deep leather armchairs round the bar, old leather tomes and worn paperbacks on the bookshelves. The yellow breakfast room is a light fresh space that opens onto a much-planted little patio where you can sit in summer. Upstairs, rooms are classically muted: eggshell walls, dark green or deep ginger carpets, some adventurously bright bedcovers or curtains, one or two good pieces of old furniture, more interesting pictures on the walls, good storage and space to sit peacefully. One pair of singles is suddenly more feminine in satiny, musliny, peachy softness. At the top, two rooms have terraces for breakast or drinks surveying miles of rooftops. Some bathrooms have been more recently renovated than others, one is still in its super 1930s mosaic outfit. All linen is bordered and monogrammed and all rooms except the smallest have double doors from the corridor. The feel of deep quilted comfort and old-style class will be cultivated but all beds are to be changed. *English spoken.*

rooms	41: 26 doubles & junior suites, 15 twins. Triples possible.
price	€ 119–€ 195.
meals	Breakfast € 8.
metro	La Muette (9), Passy (6).
RER	Boulainvilliers.
buses	22 32 52
car park	19 rue de Passy

Sabine Moisan

tel	(0)1 45 24 43 03
fax	(0)1 45 24 41 39
e-mail	trocadero-la-tour@magic.fr
web	www.trocadero-la-tour.com

300 years ago, Passy was a country village where society ladies came for the fertility-enhancing waters; now it is part of metropolitan Paris where they shop and entertain.

map 3   entry 85

Hôtel Nicolo

3 rue Nicolo, 75016 Paris

The low passage opens onto garden, sky and superb teak benches. Enter the building beyond – all is hushed as the old mosaic floor smiles at you; on your right, French Granny's sitting room, ahead, delightful staff who have loved the Nicolo for years and love its transformation. The new owner brought many-splendoured furnishings and pictures by artist friends (old engravings coloured 'in the manner of', pastels of Port Grimaud, a powerful parrot series). The bedrooms, all giving onto courtyards, are utter charmers, mixing rich far-eastern carving with contemporary lighting intelligence: lovely lacey-carved Indonesian screens have become voluptuous bedheads with original paintwork and fabric panels or birds or animals; there are unusual Dutch, French and oriental antique desks and tables; lamps are beautiful modern objects; pure new white beds have quilts in broad, rich stripes. Here are richness and purity married, and the new bathrooms are luscious too. A fascinating study in change and a super, welcoming place to stay. *Ceiling fans in all rooms. Lift access on mid-floor landings. English, German, Italian, Spanish spoken.*

Nicolo was destined to be a Maltese merchant but became a Parisian composer of light operas that enchanted Napoleonic France. One of his best-loved works was The Lottery Ticket.

rooms	28: 18 doubles, 6 twins, 4 junior suites for 4.
price	€91–€142, suites €142–€150.
meals	Breakfast €6.
metro	Passy (6), La Muette (9).
RER	Boulainvilliers.
buses	22 32
car park	Consult hotel.

Catherine and her team

tel	(0)1 42 88 83 40
fax	(0)1 42 24 45 41
e-mail	hotel.nicolo@wanadoo.fr
web	www.123france.com

Hôtel Frémiet Eiffel

6 avenue Frémiet, 75016 Paris

Rising up from the Seine, the little street is an exuberant piece of architectural symmetry dated 1913, all curves and juttings, stone garlands and fantasies. Marvellously, the Frémiet has kept the volumes and decorations of its apartment block origins and the owners are proud to declare that "guestrooms may not be rational but guests are most carefully attended to". From the lovely staircase (superb windows), each landing has a grand double door into the original vast 10ft-high apartment, now divided up. The old drawing room became a generous bedroom that glories in a curved window and balcony with river view; the former kitchen is a huge bathroom with a cockerel crowing in the tiles – a lesson in French apartment design just before society collapsed into the Great War. The old-style comfort matches the grand atmosphere: classic Louis XV and Louis XVI pieces, some built-in practicalities, up-to-date colour schemes and the occasional touch by the owner's designer daughter; all rooms are fully soundproofed; bathrooms are good, some magnificent. The welcome is high-class, too – it's a wonderful old-world place. *English, German and Spanish spoken.*

rooms	36: 18 doubles, 10 twins, 6 singles, 2 suites for 4.
price	€107–€215; suites €320.
meals	Breakfast € 11.50; lunch & dinner on request € 15–€30.
metro	Passy (6).
RER	Champ de Mars.
buses	32 72
car park	In street or garage 200m.

In the Wine Museum just up the road, deep galleries plunge into the hillside to take you through the history of French wine. Your ticket includes a tasting; you can even have lunch there.

Madame Fourmond

tel	(0)1 45 24 52 06
fax	(0)1 53 92 06 46
e-mail	hotel.fremiet@wanadoo.fr
web	bestwestern.com/fr/fremieteiffel

map 3   entry 87

Hôtel Gavarni

5 rue Gavarni, 75116 Paris

The neat little Gavarni astonishes yet again, heaving itself up on ropes of rich draperies, interesting pictures, beautiful bathrooms and superb finishes into the miniature luxury class. From its amazing ground floor of deep raspberry and yellow richness, tailormade murals and pretty breakfast room, you may expect more delights. The suites and deluxe doubles at the top are big and stunning in their jacuzzis, fine trimmings and beautiful furniture – supremely French yet never overdone. The lower you go, the smaller the rooms but the quality is the same: thick lovely carpets, finely-stitched quilts, heavily-draped curtains and good little pieces of furniture. One tiny single is as tempting as toffee in pale mauve, cream and florality with the original white marble fireplace and its ornate mirror. The triumph is those cramped little shower rooms which have gained so much space with their utterly ingenious made-to-measure red 'granite' basin unit, shower and loo at an angle. Hairdryers are still mounted outside! A superb combination of rich, strong modern style with pure traditional comfort. *Arabic, English, Filipino, German, Italian and Spanish spoken.*

The C19 Basque satirical cartoonist Chevalier adopted the name Gavarni in memory of a spectacular geological cirque in the Pyrenees that he came to love. Did he hope to be as spectacular?

rooms	25: 13 doubles, 4 twins, 4 singles, 1 suite for 4, 3 junior suites for 2.
price	€99-€200, suites €275-€450.
meals	Breakfast €12.50 + à la carte; lunch & dinner on request €15-€30.
metro	Passy (6), Trocadéro (6, 9).
RER	Boulainvilliers.
buses	22 32
car park	Garage Moderne, Rue de Passy.

Xavier Moraga

tel	(0)1 45 24 52 82
fax	(0)1 40 50 16 95
e-mail	reservation@gavarni.com
web	www.gavarni.com

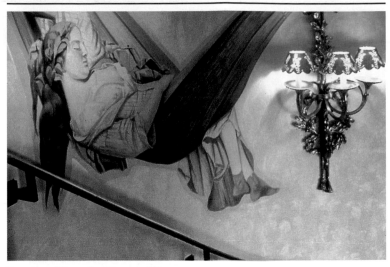

Les Jardins du Trocadéro

35 rue Benjamin Franklin, 75116 Paris

A listed 1870s building with exuberantly Napoleon III décor, it is lavish and relaxed, intimate and fun. Behind the bronze-leafed glass door, two Egyptian torch-bearers salute. Muses beckon from landing walls, musical monkeys gambol over doors, all painted by Beaux Arts students. The atmosphere is young and casual – a sweet alabaster Beatrice smiles from the desk – but efficiency and service are there, discreet and unobsequious. Lovers of the bijou will like it here, so will fans of French style. The gilded, bronze-encrusted *salon* has pure Second Empire furniture on a perfectly aged marble floor and drinks are served at a genuine bistro bar, *le zinc*. The great suite is magnificently regal in crimson and gold with matching telephone, green touches and langorous neo-classical pictures. Otherwise, don't expect big rooms but enjoy their soft generous draperies and the genuine antiques that the owners took such trouble finding – lots of ormolu trimmed Boulle-type pieces – then, surrounded by marble, luxuriate in your whirlpool bath (a double one in the suite) and fluffy bathrobe. *English and Japanese spoken.*

rooms	17: 12 doubles, 4 twins, 1 suite for 4.
price	€235-€275, suite €395.
meals	Unlimited breakfast buffet €14.50; lunch & dinner on request €15-€30.
metro	Trocadéro (6, 9).
RER	& Air France bus: Charles de Gaulle-Étoile.
buses	22 30 32 63
car park	Consult hotel.

Monsieur Chekroun

tel	(0)1 53 70 17 70
fax	(0)1 53 70 17 80
e-mail	jardintroc@aol.com
web	www.jardintroc.com

Franklin's active opposition to England greatly endeared him to France and the French government declared three whole days of national mourning when he died in 1790.

map 1   entry 89

ÉTOILE - CHAMPS ÉLYSÉES

Rue Rabelais
Place Rio de Janeiro
Rue d'Argentine

(François) Rabelais - Rio de Janeiro - Argentina

Hôtel Kléber
7 rue de Belloy, 75116 Paris

A Napoleonic wind (Emperor Napoleon III, that is, in 1870s style) blows through the Kléber depositing *trompe-l'œil* draperies, people and costumed monkeys on walls (including the artist herself, marching off with palette and parrot), a splendid glass canopy, a beautifully designed marble-tile floor and unashamedly ornate, damasked furniture. Stupendous – and saved from excess by some fine, plain oak panelling. The owners love hunting for period pieces for their four hotels, hence the rococo lamps, encrustations, kitsch paintings and lifesize statues. The suite has a beautiful roll-top desk in its generous balconied *salon*, and a kitchenette. The décor is rich in colour – reds, yellows, blues – and texture; bedding is brand new; some rooms have parquet floors; tiled or mosaic bathrooms are not big but are well designed, some with whirlpool baths; breakfast among the basement stones and swags includes cereals, cheese and eggs for a fine start to the day. Don't come for vast spaces, come for the exuberant style and the lively, cosmopolitan atmosphere where *English, Spanish, Hebrew, Japanese and Arabic are spoken.*

rooms	22: 15 doubles, 6 twins, 1 suite for 4.
price	€ 182–€ 243, suite € 304.
meals	Buffet breakfast € 13; lunch & dinner on request € 15–€ 30.
metro	Kléber (6), Boissière (6).
RER	& Air France bus: Charles de Gaulle-Étoile.
buses	22 30 82 63
car park	Consult hotel.

Kléber, soldier son of an Alsatian pastry cook, couldn't, as a commoner, hope for officer rank in the King's army but rose fast after the Revolution killed the King: he died a General under Napoleon.

Samuel Abergel

tel	(0)1 47 23 80 22
fax	(0)1 49 52 07 20
e-mail	kleberhotel@aol.com
web	www.kleberhotel.com

map 1   entry 90

Hôtel Élysées Matignon

3 rue de Ponthieu, 75008 Paris

Matignon is superb genuine 1924 — clearcut rectangles, perfectly moulded curves, bags of style and no fuss. In that stunning lobby, you will be welcomed by people who are relaxed yet sensitive to your needs. Each bedroom wall bears a large original fresco: landscapes or near-abstract still lifes, they are very proper given the original purpose of these rooms. Bathrooms have Art Deco mod cons and bevelled black and white Metro tiling (some are being renovated in pale green mosaic — Deco but new). Otherwise, there are discreet dark carpets, heavy curtains, pleasing clear colour schemes with coordinated quilted or textured bedcovers and head cushions (a bow to 1990s fashion), black metal bedside lights (another), fine inner blinds and decent storage. If far from enormous, each room has a useful lobby for minibar, cupboard and loo (except the junior suites where a larger lobby houses the extra bed). An evening venue for the Parisian 'in' crowd (11 pm to dawn), the scarlet and black Mathis Bar, newly adorned with a dancing silver and glass Belle Époque chandelier, puts on virginal white for breakfast. *English, Portuguese and Spanish spoken.*

Mansions were built here in the 1700s (the Élysée Palace, for example, for La Pompadour); in the 1800s, the 'Elysian Fields' were covered with modest houses; in the 1920s, activity was less modest...

rooms	23: 10 doubles, 9 twins, 4 junior suites.
price	€136–€198; suites €198–€218.
meals	Breakfast €9.15; lunch & dinner on request €17–€25.
metro	Franklin Roosevelt (1, 9).
RER	& Air France bus: Charles de Gaulle-Étoile.
buses	28 32 42 49 52 73 80 93
car park	Champs Elysées.

Alain Michaud & Jean-François Cornillot

tel	(0)1 42 25 73 01
fax	(0)1 42 56 01 39
e-mail	elyseesmatignon@wanadoo.fr
web	www.hotel-paris-champselysees.com

Hôtel de l'Élysée

12 rue des Saussaies, 75008 Paris

This classically, comfortably French hotel now has a big light lobby with vistas past columns and mirrors to a Napoleon III *salon* of much refinement (the 3-seat 'eavesdropper's' sofa is sheer delight) to match its hand-painted *faux marbre* stairwell, mosaic floors and antiques. It's a country-house environment with a few dramatically baroque details – a study of lamps and lights reveals some astounding gilded sprays and spiky vegetables – and the owner's collection of watercolours and engravings. Otherwise, Jouy-print walls, quilting, padding and plush are the thing. As usual, some 'standard' rooms are quite small but always with a moulded ceiling or hand-painted cupboard. Some rooms in shades of green, brown and beige are fairly sombre, others are covered in bright flowers, raspberry, apple green, mustard yellow; big deluxe corner rooms are superb with three windows; top-floor junior suites have great character – sloping ceilings, timbers, nooks, pretty décor. A place of taste and comfort, it faces the Ministry of the Interior so there's always a policeman at your door. Ask about long-stay terms for our readers. *English and German spoken.*

rooms	32: 29 doubles/twins; 1 suite, 2 junior suites. Connecting rooms.
price	€ 130–€ 220, suites € 260–€ 320.
meals	Continental-plus breakfast € 10; lunch & dinner on request € 10–€ 30.
metro	Champs Élysées Clemenceau (1, 13), Madeleine (8, 12, 14).
RER	Auber.
buses	28 32 49 52 80 83 93
car park	Hôtel Bristol.

The 'tenant' of the Place Beauvau is Interior Minister and chief of police; saussaie comes from saule = birch. In the days of birching, did the police grow their own here?

Madame Lafond

tel	(0)1 42 65 29 25
fax	(0)1 42 65 64 28
e-mail	hotel.de.l.elysees@wanadoo.fr

map 1   entry 92

Hôtel des Champs-Élysées

2 rue d'Artois, 75008 Paris

Madame Monteil inherited the hotel – and the art of hospitality – from her grandparents and parents whose delightful pre-war pictures hang here. An unpretentious façade speaks for the simple, gentle reception you will receive, in deep contrast to the nearby Champs Elysées vulgarity. And the recent Art Deco mural in the *salon* is a triumph of taste and artistic talent, as is the Roman temple behind the bar... Each room has custom-made wooden furniture; covers and curtains are often subtly coordinated English fabrics against pale pink, yellow or turquoise walls for lighter or darker effect; bedside lights are cleancut and well-placed and mirrored cupboards provide adequate storage. The small bathrooms have been renovated in smart grey, silver, black and white tiles or beige marble. Since this 'back' street may carry occasional posses of departing clubbers, all rooms (all but six give onto the street) are fully soundproofed and air-conditioned. With its quiet warmth and fresh baker's croissants and bread for breakfast, it seems to be remarkable value in an expensive neighbourhood – and exceptional human contact. *English spoken.*

Escape the frenzy with a walk in the quiet, tree-shaded Cité Odiot, reached along narrow passages off Rue Washington - it has a slight feel of Georgian London.

rooms	35: 31 doubles, 4 twins.
price	€85–€103; €120 for three.
meals	Breakfast €7.
metro	St Philippe du Roule (9), Franklin Roosevelt (1, 9).
RER	& Air France bus: Charles de Gaulle-Étoile.
buses	22 28 32 73 80 83 93
car park	Rue de Ponthieu.

Madame Monteil

tel	(0)1 43 59 11 42
fax	(0)1 45 61 00 61

Rue des Tapisseries
Rue de Rome
Impasse du Pèlerin

Tapestries - Rome - Pilgrim

Hotel Chambellan-Morgane

6 rue Keppler, 75116 Paris

The sober grey stone façade with its moulded arched doorway leads you naturally into a very feminine space of elegant classical proportions full of mouldings, mirrors and flowers. The Louis XVI *salon* and breakfast area, panelled and draped in soft yellow and blue, have a smart/relaxed appeal that is utterly French: the delightful, well-travelled lady of the house has passed her refined hand over everything. Though not enormous, the blue-carpeted bedrooms have the same classical volumes and are appropriately, unobtrusively decorated with palest pale walls, thick rich curtains and white piqué bed coverings on brand-new mattresses – it feels fresh and light with good, solid furniture and colour schemes that are variously gentle or strong but never invasive. Bath and shower rooms are simply pretty with good glass shower doors and screens, excellent fittings and accessories. The Chambellan-Morgane is small enough for every guest to receive proper personal attention and you will feel quietly relaxed in this classy house such a short way from the crazy life of the Champs Élysées. *English, German and Italian spoken.*

Interesting that, in 1864, Kepler's name should be honoured in a street that's far shorter than Galileo's, nearby: exact contemporaries, they were the founders of modern astronomy.

rooms	20: 9 doubles, 11 twins.
price	€ 145–€ 160.
meals	Continental buffet breakfast € 10; lunch & dinner on request € 10–€ 30.
metro	George V (1); Charles de Gaulle-Étoile (1, 2, 6).
RER	& Air France bus: Charles de Gaulle-Étoile.
buses	22 30 92
car park	Avenue Marceau.

Madame Christine de Lapasse

tel	(0)1 47 20 35 72
fax	(0)1 47 20 95 69
e-mail	chambellan.morgane@wanadoo.fr
web	www.hotel-paris-morgane.com

Étoile Park Hôtel

10 avenue MacMahon, 75017 Paris

The wide leafy avenue was built to Haussmann's plan in the 1860s, this smart-fronted hotel included. From some rooms they say you can see the sun rise over the Arc de Triomphe, proud and solid with its magnificent sculptures. Since arriving four years ago, Madame Leridon has, with enthusiasm and taste, transformed the sitting area into a warm unfussy 1930s space, in complete contrast with the grand exterior: natural materials – wood and stone, leather and linen – in plain colours, super pictures by Hilton McConnico (not 1930s), well-made artificial bouquets and very real cacti. Beyond is the bar with a discreet television set, then the cool light-hearted breakfast room with lively deck-chair-stripe seating and a smooth modern buffet bar. Some bedrooms have been brought back to life in muted tones with bright splashes on chairs, lamps and pictures, really good fabrics, excellent all-in-one sleek wooden units for minibar and telly and bathrooms done in enamel mosaics. The older rooms have been refreshed and are very acceptable. Well-placed and very welcoming. *Internet access. English, German and Spanish spoken.*

rooms	28: 10 doubles, 11 twins, 5 singles, 2 triples.
price	€ 84–€ 151.
meals	Breakfast € 8–€ 12; lunch & dinner on request € 15–€ 30.
metro	Charles de Gaulle-Étoile (1, 2, 6).
RER	& Air France bus: Charles de Gaulle-Étoile.
buses	30 31 73 92 93
car park	MacMahon.

Sylviane Leridon

tel	(0)1 42 67 69 63
fax	(0)1 43 80 18 99
e-mail	ephot@easynet.fr
web	www.hotel-etoilepark.com

Descended from a great Irish family, MacMahon was utterly French in his accumulation of military and political glories and titles, finishing as Field Marshal and President of the Republic in 1873.

map 1   entry 95

Hôtel Régence Étoile

24 avenue Carnot, 75017 Paris

On one of the wide leafy spokes that spin round the Arc de Triomphe, the hub of monumental Paris, the dressed-stone Régence is an utterly Right Bank hotel: smartly Empire, soberly businesslike, with a human touch. In the generous marble hall, you will be greeted by a beautiful, naked and valuable statue; the big windows are hung with pale gold curtains, properly fringed and swagged, and that fascinating black fireplace demands closer inspection. Some nice furniture and atmospheric oils of 1890s Paris grace the panelled reception end where you may be greeted by a bright and friendly young woman or by the warm, knowledgeable and polyglot manageress. The corridors are elegant blue and yellow; so are all the bedrooms: pale yellow walls, rich yellow damask curtains, blue carpets and quilts. In various shapes and sizes, they are not huge but feel plush and reassuring with their solid, traditional-style, dark polished furniture and new ivory-tiled, marble-shelved bathrooms. Rooms on the front look through wrought-iron balconies and trees to the fine buildings opposite. You will be comfortable here, and well received. *English, German and Spanish spoken.*

The Arc de Triomphe, planned by Napoleon but finished long after his fall from glory into miserable death, is 50 metres high. The view of the avenues radiating off the Étoile (star) is superb.

rooms	38: 19 doubles, 19 twins.
price	€ 120–€ 144.
meals	Buffet breakfast € 10.50.
metro	Charles de Gaulle-Étoile.
RER	& Air France bus: Charles de Gaulle-Étoile.
buses	22 30 31 43 52 73 92 93
car park	Carnot.

Madame Montagnon

tel	(0)1 58 05 42 42
fax	(0)1 47 66 78 86
e-mail	hotelregenceetoile@wanadoo.fr
web	www.parisplanet.com

Hôtel Centre Ville Étoile

6 rue des Acacias, 75017 Paris

It's tiny, stylish and different. But tiny does not mean twee, stylish does not mean daunting – and the welcome is exceptionally friendly. The shiny black desk and the 20-foot ficus tree live in a towering galleried well of light, an ingenious and original space that gives onto a semi-patio for summer breakfast and is heated by anachronistic ceramic stoves in winter. The view from the top gallery, across metal frame and curtain wall, is an engineer's delight. Based on an Art Deco black and white idea, the décor may seem severe but it has just the right dose of bright differences, such as prints from American cartoon strips. Black carpeting with slippy grey-white stripes like running water covers all. Space is well used in the smallish rooms, though storage remains limited. They can be masculine in brown and black with one red chair, or pastelly, or elegant white, cream and grey. Bathrooms are white and grey with lots of mirrors. In contrast, bright red print cloths on black tables and airy Bauhaus wire chairs enliven the basement breakfast room. With so few rooms, staff have plenty of time to be attentive, helpful – and chatty if you wish. *English spoken.*

rooms	15: 10 doubles, 5 twins.
price	€115–€151.
meals	Breakfast €9.15; lunch & dinner on request €15–€25.
metro	Argentine
RER	& Air France bus: Charles de Gaulle-Étoile.
buses	43 73 92 93
car park	24 rue des Acacias.

In 1834, Louis Philippe's heir apparent took a fast bend nearby, fell out of his carriage and was killed. Banal? Perhaps, but few crash victims have Byzantine chapels built in their memory (St Ferdinand).

Alain Michaud & Idir Nasser

tel	(0)1 58 05 10 00
fax	(0)1 47 54 93 43
e-mail	hcv@centrevillehotels.com
web	centrevillehotels.com

map 1   entry 97

ÉTOILE - PORTE MAILLOT

Hôtel Pergolèse
3 rue Pergolèse, 75116 Paris

Once past the blue doors you forget the trumpeting sculptures of nearby Arc de Triomphe for a festival of modern design where light and natural materials, custom-made furniture and minute details all add up. Édith Vidalenc works with renowned designer Rena Dumas to keep a sleek but warmly, curvaceously human hotel. Her sense of hospitality informs it all: the faithful team at reception are leagues away from the frostiness that can pass for 4-star treatment. Hilton McConnico did the pictures and the stunning carpets. Pastel tones are mutedly smart so the multi-coloured breakfast room is a slightly humorous wake-up nudge, the linen mats and fine silver a bow to tradition: not taking oneself too seriously while being really professional is the keynote here. Rooms, not vast but with good storage, are all furnished in pale wood and leather, thick curtains and soft white bedcovers: no distracting patterns or prints, just coloured plush cushions to soften. The star *Pergolèse* room (pictured) is a small masterpiece in palest apricot with a few spots of colour and a superb open bathroom. *Internet access. English, German, Italian, Japanese and Spanish spoken.*

Napoleon had the Arc de Triomphe built up there to honour every single one of the 386 generals who fought in the Republican and Imperial wars, and all their names are on it.

rooms	40: 24 doubles, 16 twins.
price	€ 170–€ 260; Pergolèse Room € 320.
meals	Breakfast € 12–€ 15; lunch & dinner on request c.€ 25.
metro	Argentine (1).
RER	& Air France bus: Porte Maillot.
buses	73 82
car park	Place St Ferdinand.

Édith Vidalenc

tel	(0)1 53 64 04 04
fax	(0)1 53 64 04 40
e-mail	hotel@pergolese.com
web	www.hotelpergolese.com

Hôtel Résidence Foch

10 rue Marbeau, 75116 Paris

Beautiful People parade beneath the carved corbels of these streets and from the solid old glass door of the hotel you can see the trees of Avenue Foch, the smartest address in Paris. Recently taken over by the silvery-elegant, ever-dynamic Nelly Rolland, the Foch is gradually being transformed into a place of sweetness and light: lemon yellow and raspberry pink in the sitting, bar and breakfast areas lit by the pretty green-growing patio, spriggy springtime paper up the stairs, good individually-chosen prints and engravings on the walls. The renovated top-floor rooms promise wonders for the rest: super-soft fabrics in gentle comforting colours – soft khaki and butter yellow, muted brick and lemon – antique furniture, stencilled borders and excellent bath or shower rooms in beige tiles with contrasting mirror frames. Rooms awaiting Nelly's magic touch have old-fashioned florals, good solid furniture, reassuring colours, bathrooms with the occasional decorative motif. One has the most marvellous private terrace. Utterly reliable, soon to be stunning. Staff welcome you with natural hospitality and relaxed good humour. *English spoken*

rooms	25: 12 doubles, 9 twins, 4 suites.
price	€ 127-€ 220, suites € 190-€ 250.
meals	Buffet breakfast € 11; lunch & dinner on request € 18-€ 26.
metro	Porte Dauphine (2), Argentine (1), Porte Maillot (1)
RER	& Air France bus: Porte Maillot; Avenue Foch.
buses	31 73 82 PC
car park	Foch or Palais des Congrès.

Horrified by the lot of the young children of working mothers, J-B Marbeau (1798-1875) founded the first crèche in 1844 and spread the idea throughout Europe.

Nelly Rolland

tel	(0)1 45 00 46 50
fax	(0)1 45 01 98 68
e-mail	residence@foch.com
web	www.foch.com

map 1   entry 99

La Villa Maillot

143 avenue de Malakoff, 75116 Paris

In the wood-panelled lobby, as everywhere in the Villa Maillot, each object asks to be admired, every picture is worthy of attention. The dynamic manageress has her priorities right, though: welcome, discretion and attention to detail come first, staff are beautifully trained and you will be very well cared for. Walk through to the big library/bar, sink into a deep sofa by the flickering fire, soak up the flower-filled light from the conservatory breakfast space and wrap yourself in quiet luxury. Bedrooms have touches of an Art Deco theme in variations on red, blue/gold or rainbow. Thick and lush is the feel, cleancut the look: softly-quilted beds of superb quality and plain-moulded walls, deep-pile carpets and big cupboards, one good picture on a white panel and at least one comfortable armchair. Up their own private stairs, suites are a positive indulgent ('Modigliani' suite pictured). As you would expect, the white and beige marble bathrooms are excellent with extras galore. And then there's the brunch, a veritable feast in a bucolic glasshouse where greenery and bird twitter transport you miles from the metropolis. *English and Spanish spoken.*

The Porte Maillot (Maillot Gate) stands at the entrance to the city of Paris - the 20 arrondissements within the historic walls - from Neuilly on the opposite bank of the Seine.

rooms	42: 29 doubles, 10 twins, 3 suites.
price	€300–€360, suites €435–€490. Weekend breaks €199 per night including brunch.
meals	Breakfast €17–€23; lunch & dinner on request €10–€30.
metro	Porte Maillot (1).
RER	Porte Maillot.
buses	73 82 PC
car park	Private garage.

Ghislaine Abinal

tel	(0)1 53 64 52 52
fax	(0)1 45 00 60 61
e-mail	resa@lavillamaillot.fr
web	www.lavillamaillot.fr

Hôtel Résidence Impériale
155 avenue Malakoff, 75116 Paris

The name is grand, the place is unfailingly approachable: Pierre Salles and his staff are enthusiastic, humorous and relaxed. He got Jean-Philippe Nuel to redesign his hotel from top to bottom, installed double-glazed double windows and air conditioning, essential for rooms over the busy avenue, custom-made furniture in natural wood to make the best use of space, touches such as original leather-covered lamps that shed a soft light and Nuel's signature wildlife pictures. Beds are firm, upholstery richly quilted, curtains thickly generous, wallpaper unobtrusive. Top-floor rooms have timbers and sloping ceilings for a bit of character; those at the back look out over a row of small private gardens and a rather lovely old curved redbrick building. The *salon* has been attractively done in clean lines of brown, yellow and ivory, ideal for the paintings showing there, and the patio is perfect with its teak tables. Conference people like it too; if you are cooped up all day in the Palais des Congrès or arrive by airport bus at the Porte Maillot, this is a nearby haven. *Internet access and tea-making kit on ground floor. English, Italian and Spanish spoken.*

rooms	37: 21 doubles, 14 twins, 2 triples.
price	€137–€195.
meals	Generous buffet breakfast €12; lunch & dinner on request €15–€20.
metro	Porte Maillot (1).
RER	& Air France bus: Porte Maillot.
buses	73 82 PC
car park	Palais des Congrès.

Pierre Salles	
tel	(0)1 45 00 23 45
fax	(0)1 45 01 88 82
e-mail	res.imperiale@wanadoo.fr
web	www.paris-charming-hotels.com

Malakoff was a bastion at Sebastopol that fell to Marshal MacMahon in the Crimean War after he (not Julius Caesar) had declared famously "J'y suis, j'y reste".

map 1   entry 101

Hôtel Regent's Garden
6 rue Pierre Demours, 75017 Paris

This mansion was built by Napoleon III for his personal doctor and the 1850s Grand Style still lingers. Coming in from the leafy courtyard carpark, watch for the chandelier, a period piece in silver bronze with mauve glass danglers and a great crystal ball. Dazzling. Then stucco and columns, drapes, tassels and fringes, gilded tripod tables and solid button chairs in a red-and-yellow pallette. But look further and discover the wonderful garden, a riot of shrubberies, flowerbeds, creepers and acacias where you can enjoy the contrast – garden-facing rooms are particularly desirable. Bedrooms, all splendidly different – some really big, even the smallest very comfortable – have Louis XVI or Victorian furniture with the occasional fine piece, good designer florals or damask or Jouy prints in red and yellow, blue and white, or a lovely lively green, decent armchairs, a sense of quiet old-fashioned confidence and padded space. Bathrooms, gradually being renovated, are excellent too. Last but first, the staff are friendly and competent and do not indulge in Victorian delirium. *Internet access. One no-smoking floor. English, Spanish spoken.*

The designer motto of Napoleon III's day was 'Trop n'est pas assez' (Too much is not enough). Compare with our minimalist 'Less is more' (Moins c'est plus).

rooms	39: 22 doubles, 11 twins, 6 triples.
price	€ 117.80–€ 242, triples € 184–€ 255.
meals	Buffet breakfast € 11.
metro	Ternes (2), Charles de Gaulle-Étoile (1, 2, 6) & Air France bus.
RER	Charles de Gaulle-Étoile.
buses	30 31 43 92 93
car park	Hotel or Ternes.

Alain Condy & Sylvie Le Guellaut

tel	(0)1 45 74 07 30
fax	(0)1 40 55 01 42
e-mail	hotel.regents.garden@wanadoo.fr
web	www.hotel-paris-garden.com

Hôtel Flaubert
19 rue Rennequin, 75017 Paris

The Schneiders' campaign to renovate and brighten the Flaubert proceeds apace: in the bedrooms vibrant blue and yellow, crimson and paisley march alongside Italian wicker furniture – it's light and not at all overbearing. There is always a table and one or two chairs or a stool, even where the space is limited; much attention has been paid to details like lighting and new tap fittings; bathrooms are good and the larger rooms have plenty of storage. The Schneiders are also tending the Flaubert's surpassing asset, its miniature jungle, a long courtyard between two buildings connected by stairs and bridges festooned with greenery and flowers that change colour each season. This could be the depths of Normandy, the great novelist Gustave Flaubert's home county, and it is most un-Parisian to walk through the bushes and up to your room under the eaves (you can take the lift, of course). The breakfast room, with its big windows onto the street, has bentwood chairs, floral cushions and Provençal tiles to prolong the country feel and there's a pretty new sitting space by the other window. Altogether excellent value. *English spoken.*

rooms	41: 27 doubles, 9 twins, 4 singles, 1 triple.
price	€90–€130.
meals	Buffet breakfast €8.
metro	Ternes (2), Pereire (3).
RER	& Air France bus: Charles de Gaulle-Étoile; Pereire.
buses	30 31 43 84 92 93
car park	Opposite hotel.

In 1682, Rennequin built the magnificent Machine de Marly which, for 120 years, propelled water up to the great fountains at Versailles using 14 wheels and 221 pumps.

Monsieur & Madame Schneider

tel	(0)1 46 22 44 35
fax	(0)1 43 80 32 34
e-mail	paris@hotelflaubert.com
web	www.hotelflaubert.com

map 1   entry 103

Hôtel de Banville
166 boulevard Berthier, 75017 Paris

Deliciously Parisian, the Banville has the elegance of inherited style and the punch of ultra-modern fittings (the sober stone corridors and cherry-red, brass-knobbed doors are fantastically numbered and lit from below ground). You feel welcomed into a private château where the family make their own *pâté* for light suppers and gilt-edged Old Masters supervise the gracious *salon*. The owners' bedroom designs are wondrous. *Marie*, in subtle tones from palest eggshell to rich red loam, has a gauzily-canopied bed, a delicious little terrace (Eiffel Tower view) and a brilliant bathroom with thick curtains for soft partitioning; *Amélie* is sunnily feminine in pale yellow and soft ginger; the three *Pastourelles* are freshly countrified in gingham and old wood; *Banville* is another exceptional mix of modern comforts, warm fabrics and history-laden wood. The other rooms, full of light, gentle colours and intimacy, have an airy touch, perfectly-chosen modern and period furniture and good bathrooms. Staff are unerringly delightful – hospitality could have been born here. *Good public transport to all parts of Paris. English, German, Italian, Spanish spoken.*

rooms	38: 37 doubles/twins, 1 apartment.
price	€ 113–€ 187; apartment € 250.
meals	Continental buffet breakfast € 11; light meals € 5–€ 20.
metro	Porte de Champerret (3), Pereire (3).
RER	Pereire.
buses	92 84 93 PC
car park	Rue de Courcelles.

Théodore de Banville, a 19th-century poet who was neither a materialist nor a romantic, had a noble passion: "to clothe my ideas in a perfect form of beauty and technical mastery".

Marianne Moreau

tel	(0)1 42 67 70 16
fax	(0)1 44 40 42 77
e-mail	hotelbanville@wanadoo.fr
web	www.hotelbanville.fr

Hôtel de la Jatte

4 boulevard du Parc, Île de la Grande Jatte, 92200 Neuilly sur Seine

A "charming small business hotel" is what the owners call the Jatte: it is just that. On an island in the leafiest, exclusivest suburb of Paris looking at the River Seine, its trees, peaceful houseboats and a less peaceful bridge, this is a place for fresh-air lovers. The light from the river washes over the super Art Deco building and into the big brown *salon*. On weekdays, the island throbs with the head offices of famous designers and couturiers and the Jatte's sober renovation has been done to suit their visitors: it is cleancut but not cold, has old books, intriguing oil paintings and skinny designer lamps. Breakfast is in the glassed-over courtyard with plain furniture and a super collection of old clocks and craftsmen's signs on the walls. Bedrooms, all very much alike, come in various colours and sizes (indicated by the number of gold squares in the bedhead!). Walls are plain ochre, ginger, red or grey, furniture is custom-made in finely-finished dark wood, curtains are high-quality thick stripes, bathrooms are new and good. The suites, ideal for families, have private doors from the courtyard where birds sing. *English and Spanish spoken.*

rooms	69: 50 doubles, 16 twins, 3 junior suites.
price	€ 106–€ 166, suites € 196.
meals	Breakfast € 10.
metro	Pont de Neuilly (1).
RER	Grande Arche de la Défense.
buses	82 93 163 164
car park	On street.

Arnaud Laurence

tel	(0)1 46 24 32 62
fax	(0)1 46 40 77 31
e-mail	paris@hoteldelajatte.com
web	www.hoteldelajatte.com

The Grande Jatte Island is worth a visit: for exercise, there are long leafy walks or energetic bicycling, tennis or bowls; for your reward, a choice of little riverside restaurants 'with their feet in the water'.

map 3   entry 105

OPÉRA - MADELEINE - GRANDS BOULEVARDS

Rue de la Victoire
Rue Montorgueil
Rue de la Tour des Dames
Rue Vide-Gousset

Victory - Mount Pride - Ladies' Tower - Pickpocket

New Orient Hôtel

16 rue de Constantinople, 75008 Paris

The New Orient (Constantinople may have something to do with the name – no-one knows) is pretty, original and fun. Behind a superbly renovated bottle-green frontage flanked by carriage lamps with ivy geraniums pouring off the windowsills, the warm, attractive owners display their love of trawling country-house sales for furniture, pictures and mirrors and the mix of styles is sheer delight – Louis XVI, 1900s, Art Deco... There are brass beds and carved beds, one with little columns, one with lovely inlay and matching dressing table. Unfortunately, beds in sales don't come in pairs so twin rooms have new, matching bedheads but there may be a little marble washstand or a pretty table to compensate and everywhere bright oriental-type or Mediterranean fabrics. The ground floor houses a painted telephone box and a carved dresser, a piano and a set of light country watercolours while a fine grandfather clock supervises the breakfast area with its rattan tables and pink/green cloths. A thoroughly human, pleasing place. *The mid-floor lift landings are narrow and awkward to negotiate with luggage. English, Arabic, German, Hindi and Italian spoken.*

rooms	30: 20 doubles, 10 twins.
price	€72–€110.
meals	Breakfast €0.
metro	Villiers (2, 3), Europe (3).
RER	Opéra-Auber.
buses	30 53
car park	Europe.

Catherine & Sepp Wehrlé

tel	(0)1 45 22 21 64
fax	(0)1 42 93 83 23
e-mail	new.orient.hotel@wanadoo.fr
web	www.hotel-paris-orient.com

In the Orsay Museum is Monet's unforgettable painting of the Gare St Lazare, flooded with steam and smoke and blurred blue light. Its raw realism caused a scandal at the time for being 'inappropriate'.

map 1   entry 106

Le Lavoisier

21 rue Lavoisier, 75008 Paris

The recently renovated Lavoisier is smoothly, frill-lessly beautiful and so calm: as you step through the door the busy streets die away and softness takes over. Here is the casual elegance of muted warm colours, fine natural materials and original portraits; antique and modern pieces are good neighbours, squidgy sofas lie alongside wrought-iron banisters, a darkly intimate bar hides at the back, tempting you to a pre-dinner drink, a dash of humour speaks from the breakfast-room mural. Traditional, with the designer touch of custom-made black wooden furniture plus the odd clever *brocante* find, the biggish bedrooms are immaculate, their tall windows clothed in thick, rich curtains, bathrooms perfect in grey and white with deep moulded friezes and loads of towels. Young, eager, helpful staff and fresh flowers on the reception desk are welcome sights after a day in the city and although the daytime buzz is constant, there's good double glazing and the little street is quiet at night – no raucous cafés. It's a thoroughly civilised place, twinned with the St Grégoire and the Tourville. *English, Italian, Japanese and Spanish spoken.*

Do walk to Place de la Madeleine and visit the most amazing public lavatories in Paris: Art Nouveau moulded doors and stained-glass windows, all hidden beneath the pavement there.

rooms	30: 26 doubles/twins, 3 junior suites, 1 suite for 4.
price	€199-€245, suites €245-€385.
meals	Continental-plus breakfast €12; lunch & dinner on request €15-€30.
metro	St Augustin (9).
RER	Auber.
buses	32 84
car park	Consult hotel.

Ludovic Peressini

tel	(0)1 53 30 06 06
fax	(0)1 53 30 23 00
e-mail	info@hotellavoisier.com
web	www.hotellavoisier.com

Hôtel du Ministère

31 rue de Surène, 75008 Paris

The Ministère is in transit and transformation. The vast ground-floor space already displays the hand of the Chekroun-Abergel family, the new owners. They bring elaborate touches such as the curlicued, gilt-trimmed stair rail, the oak panelling, the coy little statues and carvings, the red-upholstered and tasselled *salon* spreading its riches beneath the glass canopy in the centre. Here you have space and light for breakfast, reading, enjoying a drink from the bar, and even two meeting rooms. The bedrooms are a mixture of refurbished and old-style décor still waiting for the family's attention. Rooms at the top have that warm old-beams personality, quirky corners, carved beds and good Jouy-type fabrics. Everywhere, you will find French period furniture alongside more rustic pieces, built-in headboards or ladder-back country beds, a mix of grey marble or beige-tiled or old-style flowery bathrooms, plush chairs and rich dark curtains, often in red and cream. There's the odd jacuzzi or antique mirror; it is all comfortable, clean and quiet; and the original stained-glass windows on the staircase are wonderful. *English and Italian spoken.*

rooms	28: 8 doubles, 10 twins, 6 triples, 4 singles.
price	€105–€218.
meals	Buffet breakfast €11; lunch & dinner on request €15, €30.
metro	Madeleine (8, 12, 14); Concorde (1, 8, 12).
RER	Opéra–Auber.
buses	24 42 84 94
car park	Madeleine.

Madeleine Twena-Abergel

tel	(0)1 42 66 21 43
fax	(0)1 42 66 96 04
e-mail	hministere@aol.com
web	www.ministerehotel.com

Strangely, and despite the spelling, since 1652 the street name has meant that this is the 'highway' to the distant suburb of Suresnes. Seems a long way and a long time.

map 1   entry 108

Hôtel La Sanguine
6 rue de Surène, 75008 Paris

Through a little lobby and up one flight to a house of flowers and easy friendliness. You will be welcomed by delightful, energetic people and Tokyo the tiny sausage dog, all family or long-standing staff. The atmosphere is one of quiet country-style comfort. The desk and a couple of classical statues overlook the floral breakfast tables and through to a little green patio: hard to believe that the powers of this world – ministers, fashion gurus, ambassadors – live round the corner. Carpets are thick, rooms are fresh and bright with good designer fabrics, wood or cane furniture, discreet personality, properly-equipped marble bathrooms and umpteen *sanguine* (red-chalk drawings) to lend gentle interest; the little singles take one back to childhood and Beatrix Potter. Service here is infinitely human and attentive: in season, the owners make jam for your breakfast with fruit from their orchard; Monsieur bakes your breakfast croissant then irons your monogrammed towels; Madame is full of good advice on where to shop and what to see. Exceptionally welcoming. *Wines sold for private consumption. Laundry service. No lift, four floors. English spoken.*

The brilliant artist, poet, author, film-maker Jean Cocteau, darling of the theatrical/poetical set between the World Wars, had a mother too: he used to stay here when visiting her in Rue d'Anjou.

rooms	31: 18 doubles, 5 twins, 8 singles.
price	€85–€139, including breakfast.
meals	Breakfast included.
metro	Madeleine (8, 12, 14), Concorde (1, 8, 12)
RER	Auber.
buses	42 52 84 94
car park	Madeleine.

Monsieur & Madame Plumerand

tel	(0)1 42 65 71 61
fax	(0)1 42 66 96 77
e-mail	hotelsanguine@free.fr

Hôtel Newton Opéra

11 bis rue de l'Arcade, 75008 Paris

The Newton's hallmark? A pretty flask of mandarine liqueur and two tiny goblets in your room. Attention to detail and care for your every comfort are priorities here: the management will enfold you in soft vanilla elegance and you should want for nothing. The big peach plush *salon* with period pieces on oriental rugs is a good place to read the papers; the breakfast room is a classic stone vault with high-backed chairs and a generous buffet (including teas by Hédiard), the prints are reminders of the artistic heyday of the 1900s. Bedrooms are not big but very attractive in their colourful dress of sunshine yellow, peach pink or cool blue, the furniture Louis XVI or polished rustic with a lyre-back chair or two, a long gilt-framed mirror, new bedding... and a modem socket; the bathrooms prettily-tiled with magnifiying glasses... and power showers. Two rooms have private, shrubbed balconies with tables and loungers; book early, they are much coveted. Or try the bargain weekend offer with room, champagne and a night out in the price. It's all cosy, friendly and very sweet. *Internet access. English, German, Italian, Spanish spoken.*

rooms	31: 23 doubles, 7 twins, 1 triple.
price	€ 150–€ 200.
meals	Buffet breakfast € 13, Hédiard tray € 30–€ 40.
metro	Madeleine (8, 12, 14), Havre-Caumartin (3, 9).
RER	Auber.
buses	22 27 42 52 53 66 Roissybus
car park	Rue Chauveau Lagarde.

Monsieur Simian, Madame Tobrouki

tel	(0)1 42 65 32 13
fax	(0)1 42 65 30 90
e-mail	newtonopera@easynet.fr
web	www.hotel-newton-opera.com

La Madeleine took time to find its religious feet: started in 1764, stopped during the Revolution, named Temple of Fame by Napoleon, it was finally consecrated in 1842.

map 1   entry 110

Hôtel Langlois-Croisés

63 rue St Lazare, 75009 Paris

Built as a bank in 1870, this splendid building soon became a hotel and the best rooms carry wonderful legacies of the days of rich dark furniture and log fires: ceramic and marble fireplaces, superbly crafted cupboards, carved alcoves – one room even has a 'gazebo'. Not all rooms are as spectacular but choice ornaments are placed here and there and bathrooms are fine, some enormous. Curtains and coverings fit too: heavy velvets, lots of red, some pretty pastel piqués, and rooms are big enough to take it. In the attractive ground-floor breakfast room there's yet another fireplace and a lovely antique bird cage housing two plaster birds – a nice gesture. This is a generous house and the owner wants deeply to keep the building's historical character (others would have ripped out 'all that old stuff' ages ago), only looking for furniture with 1900-1930 lines. Madame Bojena, a gentle and efficient presence, has known and loved the place for years. Previously called the Croisés, it became the Langlois after featuring as that in the film *Charade* in 2001. There's double glazing, though the traffic dies down after 8 pm. *English, Polish, Turkish spoken.*

Henri Langlois, saviour of miles of maltreated film after the war, founded the much-envied Cinémathèque on those reels and became its rather tyrannical prince until deposed by the great Malraux.

rooms	27: 20 doubles, 4 twins, 3 suites.
price	€77–€94, suites €118.
meals	Continental buffet breakfast €7.50.
metro	Trinité – d'Estienne d'Orves (12).
RER	Auber.
buses	26 32 42 43 68 81
car park	300m: consult hotel.

Madame Bojena

tel	(0)1 48 74 78 24
fax	(0)1 49 95 04 43
e-mail	hotel-des-croises@wanadoo.fr

Hôtel Opéra Richepanse

14 rue du Chevalier de Saint George, 75001 Paris

At the centre of a throbbingly busy shopping and business district, the cool 1930s look and courteous welcome of the Richepanse promise rest and quiet in proper four-star fashion. The marquetry, the panelling, the smooth suede furniture and the stylish mouldings of the lobby/*salon* were all custom-designed for the deep renovations done by the new owner. It feels clean-cut and rich. There's a minor concession to things more ancient in the atmospheric stone vault where the floor is blue, the marble bistro tables shine and the sumptuous breakfast buffet calls. Bedrooms are a good size, some are enormous. They have blue carpets, pale yellow sponged walls, clean-limbed polished 1930s-style furniture and excellent thick textured fabrics for straight-hung curtains and well-fitting bedcovers – no swags, no frills, no fuss. This gives space to appreciate the interesting reproductions that draw the eye and even, in the magnificent great suites, original paintings. Bathrooms are, of course, superb with the latest in basin design, triple mirrors and simple, smart tiling. Modern comforts, old-style attention and service. *Pets €13. English, German, Spanish spoken.*

rooms	38: 20 doubles, 15 twins, 3 suites.
price	€224–€298, suites €427–€534.
meals	Breakfast €13–€18.
metro	Madeleine (8, 14).
RER	Auber.
buses	42 52 84 94
car park	Madeleine.

Madame Laporte & Monsieur Jacques	
tel	(0)1 42 60 36 00
fax	(0)1 42 60 13 03
e-mail	richyepanseotel@wanadoo.fr
web	www.richepanse.com

General Richepanse so brutally quelled a black rebellion in the Caribbean in 1802 that in 2002 the socialist mayor of Paris renamed this street after a highly accomplished 18th-century 'black gentleman'.

map 2   entry 112

Le Stendhal Hôtel

22 rue Danielle Casanova, 75002 Paris

The Stendhal is a house of taste and luxury whose attentive owners choose period furniture, lamps and pictures individually – a brilliant mix of classic and modern – where at each visit the informed art lover enquires about new acquisitions. In the intimate, warmly panelled lobby and bar/*salon*, smiles are spontaneous, books and soft leather summon, quiet music relaxes. Rooms are biggish, even the smallest are very adequate, and there's plenty of storage. Attractive décors – blue and yellow, brick-red and fawn, some strong, some sober – are done with fine new fabrics and fabulous old mirrors and the *Stendhal* room is, of course, deep red all over with black splashes and powerful atmosphere (the great author of *Le Rouge et le Noir* died here in 1842). All rooms have a lobby for soundproofing, those at the back overlook someone else's supremely elegant inner courtyard (we are in one of the ritziest parts of Paris) and bathrooms spread great white tiles, rich-coloured basins and pretty friezes or mosaics over their generosity. Choose fresh orange or grapefruit juice for breakfast and recline in the lap of pure Paris. *English, German, Spanish spoken.*

Danièle Casanova was a fiercely committed resistance fighter during the Second World War occupation of Paris, who was deported and died in the camps in 1943.

rooms	21: 13 doubles, 5 twins, 2 junior suites, 1 suite.
price	€233–€292, suites €301–€364.
meals	Continental-plus breakfast €16.50; lunch & dinner on request €15–€45.
metro	Opéra (3, 7, 8), Pyramides (7, 14), Tuileries (1).
RER	Auber.
buses	21 27 29 68 81 95
car park	Place Vendôme.

Anne Onno

tel	(0)1 44 58 52 52
fax	(0)1 44 58 52 00
e-mail	H1610@accor-hotels.com

Hôtel Favart
5 rue de Marivaux, 75002 Paris

The Favart's splendid reception rooms are pure *Vie Parisienne* with their columns, velvet and superb curly stair rail – right and proper, given its elaborate neo-classical neighbour, the Opéra Comique (Salle Favart). The breakfast room is also greenly grand, mirrored and rich. But the people who greet you are unpretentious and friendly. one understands why generations of a cosmopolitan collection of clients keep coming. Off the newly salmon-pink corridors, good-sized bedrooms, some still being renovated, are classic in style with reproduction furniture, plush, swags and moiré. Each now has a brass knocker and an oil painting of a well-known scene. On the first floor street side you can enjoy living under original beams and behind gently arched windows (those glaziers feared no challenge) that face the rising sun and the Salle Favart; and all is quiet once the theatre-goers have left. Even the bathrooms have personality, be they almost competely mirrored or done with amazing blue blotches. Comfort, character and a sense of service are the keynotes here, in among the great theatres and the much sung boulevards. *English, Italian and Spanish spoken.*

rooms	37: 18 doubles, 14 twins, 5 triples.
price	€85–€130, including breakfast.
meals	Breakfast included.
metro	Richelieu-Drouot (8, 9).
RER	Opéra-Auber.
buses	20 39 48
car park	Boulevard des Italiens.

Having started life as a pastry-cook, 18th-century dramatic author Charles Simon Favart created the musical comedy (yes, two centuries ago) and was hugely popular for half a century.

Éric Champetier
tel	(0)1 42 97 59 83
fax	(0)1 40 15 95 58
e-mail	favart.hotel@wanadoo.fr
web	www.hotel-paris-favart.com

map 2   entry 114

Hôtel Chopin

10 boulevard Montmartre, (46 passage Jouffroy), 75009 Paris

So Parisian! Built in 1846 in a typical shopping arcade, the Chopin has always been an hotel, the piano not tuned and the great green pot planted in the airy lobby since Chinoiserie was 'in'. Smiles are freely given, people are pleased to see you, Monsieur Bidal's grandmother's watercolours add class to the welcoming breakfast room. Unusually quiet, all rooms give onto courtyards and low rooftops, the most stunning being the zinc expanses over the waxworks museum (sleep deeply above bloody scenes of French Revolution): the *Salle des Papillons* looks like a medieval apsed chapel, the glass roof of the arcade like a vast upturned hull. Most rooms are a good size for the price; bathrooms are modern, simple and functional – one has an attic boudoir corner with chair. Stairs and corridors are elegant with rich green carpet, salmon grasspaper walls, nicely-framed prints and some fine table lamps. Bedrooms have vibrant colour schemes (deep salmon, bright yellow or raspberry walls, rich green carpets and matching upholstery), simple, pretty furniture and firm foam mattresses. A supremely friendly, good-value hotel. *English, Spanish and Italian spoken.*

rooms	36: 13 doubles, 12 twins, 5 singles (1 with separate wc), 6 triples.
price	€63–€94.
meals	Continental buffet breakfast €7.
metro	Richelieu-Drouot (8, 9), Grands Boulevards (8, 9).
RER	Auber.
buses	49 67 74 85
car park	Rue Chauchat.

Walking tours of these ancestors of the shopping mall are organised and there are some fascinating trades in the arcade - an antique walking stick and cane specialist, for example.

Philippe Bidal

tel	(0)1 47 70 58 10
fax	(0)1 42 47 00 70

Hôtel Pulitzer Opéra

23 rue du Faubourg Montmartre, 75009 Paris

The contrast between the noisy, colourful, car-hooting, populous shopping and cabaret scene on the street and the interior of the smooth new Pulitzer, full of space and light and peace, is almost miraculous. It is modern and streamlined, warmed by expanses of redwood panelling, enlivened by the little garden passage through the centre. The breakfast space downstairs is another contrast, after the breadth and columns of the lobby: a long narrow well-modernised cellar vault in cream and blue with a tiny blue pinlight over each table and the feel of a Pullman dining car full of travel nostalgia, though you un-nostalgically collect your coffee from a mechanical *Autobar*. Bedrooms, half of them over the street, half over the patio, are all in the same style: wooden floors, spreading redwood panels against pale yellow walls, big windows where possible, thick dark green gold-flecked cotton draperies, decent storage and a reasonable amount of space. Bathrooms are mostly pale sage and eau-de-nil with proper mirrors and sensible shelf space. No fuss or fringes – but a friendly young welcome. Small pets €23. *English, Spanish, Arabic, Swedish, Turkish spoken.*

rooms	44: 6 singles, 11 doubles, 26 twins, 1 suite.
price	€140–€217, suite €260–€265.
meals	Buffet breakfast €12; lunch & dinner on request €15–€25.
metro	Grands Boulevards (8, 9).
RER	Auber.
buses	74
car park	Drouot.

Contrary to general belief, the grands boulevards were not Baron Haussmann's doing: it was Louis XIV who tore down part of Paris to open these avenues to give his courtiers strolling space.

Yolanda Herrero

tel	(0)1 53 34 98 10
fax	(0)1 53 34 00 07
e-mail	info@hotelpulitzer.com
web	www.hotelpulitzer.com

map 2   entry 116

Villa Fénelon

23 rue Buffault, 75009 Paris

Why Villa? Possibly because of the wonderful shrubbery between the two 19th-century townhouses that make up the hotel. You enter via what was the great carriage porch, framed by pilastered mirrored arches and leading to the old stable yard, now the garden. Soft lighting, comfortable armchairs and oriental rugs soften the space, Max the owner's bright little Westie guards it; there's a more intimate *salon* onto the street, one breakfast space beyond it in dark blue and gold, and another with teak furniture, a rich tapestry and a big garden window (remember, breakfast is included!). Bedrooms are furnished in repro Louis XVI and a motley choice of colour schemes in florals and stripes: quite a lot of pale tangerine and ginger, giving lift and personality, mirrors on sliding or accordeon cupboard doors. Bathrooms, some with more mirror panels, could do with refreshment. The little street is quiet – there's a synagogue opposite – though two main thoroughfares pass nearby so there could be traffic noise, but it feels very peaceful inside. It's good value and convenient for the Gare du Nord. *English and Spanish spoken.*

Archbishop Fénelon, a brilliant teacher and preacher, was described by Sainte Beuve as "that tall, thin, big-nosed man with eyes whence fire and spirit flow in torrents".

rooms	38: 14 doubles, 12 twins, 11 singles, 1 triple.
price	€70–€105 including breakfast.
meals	Breakfast included.
metro	Cadet (7), Notre Dame de Lorette (12).
RER	Auber, Gare du Nord.
buses	26 32 42 43 67 74 85
car park	Rue Mayran.

Eric Champetier

tel	(0)1 48 78 32 18
fax	(0)1 48 78 38 15
e-mail	villa.fenelon@wanadoo.fr
web	www.hotel-paris-fenelon.com

Hôtel Français

13 rue du 8 mai 1945, 75010 Paris

That name was graven in stone and those great doors carved in 1882 when this venerable hotel was built, just after the double spread of triumphant east-bound railway station opposite. An old-fashioned sense of service has lasted too, from a consistently smiling, easy welcome in the high entrance hall to an iron, ironing board and clothes line for every room. There are luminous stained-glass windows on the proud staircase and a reproduction Roman-head water-spout in the great new covered 'patio' space where a remarkable buffet is wheeled in on ice-cream trolleys. Bedrooms come in various sizes and styles, some just renovated – pale yellow walls, soft red or green-print quilts, pleasing red-trimmed furniture (pictured) – some still fairly urban-rustic in their 80s beige/brown décor and laminate fittings; they are all to be gradually brought to the same standard; corridors are being smartened this winter but cleanliness is the owners' priority. Half the rooms give onto the utterly quiet 'landscaped' courtyard. You are 300m from the Gare du Nord for Eurostar, Charles de Gaulle and other European connections. *English and Spanish spoken. Internet access.*

rooms	71: 41 doubles, 10 twins, 20 triples.
price	€77–€111. Children in parents' room free.
meals	Breakfast buffet €8.
metro	Gare de l'Est (4, 5, 7).
RER	Gare du Nord.
buses	30 31 32 39 46 47 54 56 65
car park	Consult hotel.

Jocelyne & Yves Bienvenu

tel	(0)1 40 35 94 14
fax	(0)1 40 35 55 40
e-mail	hotelfrancais@wanadoo.fr
web	www.hotelfrancais.com

Hitler committed suicide on 3rd May 1945 and the war in Europe officially ended on the 8th, since when hundreds of French streets and squares have saluted this event - precisely.

map 2   entry 118

MONTMARTRE

Rue du Ruisseau
Rue du Baigneur
Impasse Grosse Bouteille

Stream - Bather - Big Bottle

Hôtel des Arts

5 rue Tholozé, 75018 Paris

That little blue, plant-filled face on the steep narrow street is deceptive – the door opens onto a big reception space with all the ingredients of a personal welcome: oriental rugs on new tiles, long glass-fronted oak bookcase (with books), old stones and smiling faces – reflected in a wall of mirrors and shiny ceiling fabric (to be changed very soon). On the right, a thoroughly French-bourgeois *salon* with family antiques, interesting pictures and peace. This is indeed a family hotel and both quiet-spoken generations will receive you in simple style. Rooms are a reasonable size for two stars and in the same vein: simple and uncluttered, with good colour schemes (e.g. warm ginger and black carpeting, red and yellow tartan fabric), interior sprung mattresses and a sense of quiet comfort – nothing plush, nothing dated. Some bathrooms have been renovated in crazy mosaic tiling, others are fine in their older beige garb. All the paintings are by Montmartre artists and the basement breakfast area is almost a gallery for Roland Dubuc – as well as displaying an excellent-value cold buffet. *English spoken.*

rooms	50: 22 doubles, 28 twins.
price	€58–€78.
meals	Buffet breakfast €6.50
metro	Blanche (2), Abbesses (12),
RER	Gare du Nord.
buses	30 54 68 74 80 Montmartrobus
car park	Impasse Blanche.

Philippe Lameyre

tel	(0)1 46 06 30 52
fax	(0)1 46 06 10 83
e-mail	hotel.arts@wanadoo.fr
web	www.arts-hotel-paris.com

Montmartre - Mount of Mars? Mercury? Martyrs? Famous for slender virtues, it has seriously religious origins: the abbey was built in 1133 and noble families fought to put their daughters on the Abbess's throne of power.

map 2   entry 119

Hôtel Prima Lepic
29 rue Lepic, 75018 Paris

It's a fascinating warren of a place, built round three little courtyards, where all rooms are differently, deliciously countrified – like staying at granny's cottage with that dazzlingly 1920s hall floor, light flowery wallpapers, lace and bows, draped canopies, little old tables and cast-iron conservatory furniture among the plant life for breakfast or afternoon tea. The place is totally wedded to Montmartre: balustrades, floors and doors at all angles, village life bustling among the little shops outside. And the new owners, passionate about the Lepic, have been renovating hard in all faithfulness to the country inn theme: brass lamps and big gilt-framed mirrors by muslin canopies, floral friezes, Jouy prints and spriggy quilts – while the new bathrooms, some with startling red floors, are still smallish and functional but more up to date. The largest rooms have grand double doors, two windows, perhaps a balcony with long, long view or a marble fireplace... But other rooms are good value too. And afternoon teas are planned for winter-time, with the occasional home-made cake for weary travellers. An excellent place with delightful staff. *English spoken.*

General Lepic knew how to follow the wind of fortune: he fought brilliantly for Napoleon and was made a Baron, then turned royalist and was made a Count by King Louis XVIII.

rooms	38: 10 doubles, 20 doubles/twins, 5 singles, 3 suites.
price	€78–€123, suites €150–€170.
meals	Buffet breakfast €7.50; afternoon tea available.
metro	Blanche (2), Abbesses (12).
RER	Gare du Nord.
buses	30 54 68 74 80 Montmartrobus
car park	Impasse Blanche - consult hotel.

Martine Bourgeon

tel	(0)1 46 06 44 64
fax	(0)1 46 06 66 11
e-mail	reservations@hotel-prima-lepic.com
web	www.paris-hotel-village.com

Terrass' Hôtel

12 rue Joseph de Maistre, 75018 Paris

The Terrass' is the biggest (and highest) hotel in this book but its owner has so proper an idea of receiving guests that the atmosphere is as genuinely warm as at his smaller hotels. Antiques and tapestries, bronzes and old prints remove any sense of cold grandeur, a pianist plays in the club-like bar every evening, the breakfast buffet is a masterpiece in a room flooded with the light that pours up the hill, the chef has an excellent reputation and you may have the fine-weather privilege of eating on the seventh-floor terrace looking across the whole city — this is four-star class indeed. The junior suites are superb (one has a private terrace): big and light with windows that fling you across the greenery of Montparnasse cemetery, pale modern furniture and lovely matchings of green, blue, raspberry, beige, yellow textured fabrics. Amazing-wonderful bathrooms too, with original layouts, pretty tiles, possibly a jacuzzi. Other rooms have a more classic Louis XVI cane style and, of course, less space but all have delectable colours, different pictures and that rich, soft welcome of real taste and attention to detail. *English and German spoken.*

rooms	100: 45 doubles, 40 twins, 15 junior suites.
price	€ 194–€ 256, suites €311
meals	Breakfast buffet included. Restaurant La Terrasse: €20–€ 100.
metro	Place de Clichy (2, 13), Blanche (2).
RER	Gare du Nord.
buses	80 95 Montmartrobus
car park	Abbesses.

Simone Branco de Verra &
Marie-Caroline Brunel

tel	(0)1 46 06 72 85
fax	(0)1 42 52 29 11
e-mail	reservation@terrass-hotel.com
web	terrass-hotel.com

Joseph de Maistre was so ardent a Catholic and adversary of the French Revolution that he developed a theocratic system to restore the power of King, Pope and God in one fell swoop.

map 2   entry 121

WHAT'S IN THE BACK OF THE BOOK? ...

USEFUL VOCABULARY

Some useful words and expressions:

Bolster/Pillow — *Un Traversin/Un Oreiller*

Blanket — *Une Couverture*

Towel — *Une Serviette*

Tea; herb tea — *Un Thé; Une Infusion*

Ice — *De la glace*

Ice-cream, Mirror — *Une Glace*

Glass — *Un Verre*

Coat hangers — *Des Cintres*

Light bulb, Blister — *Une Ampoule*

Sticking plaster — *Du Sparadrap*

Soap; Shampoo — *Du Savon; Du Shampooing*

Lavatory paper — *Du Papier toilette*

Fan — *Un Ventilateur*

Out of order; broken — *En panne; cassé*

Stuck — *Coincé*

The room is too small/big/noisy/quiet/expensive/cheap.
La chambre est trop petite /grande bruyante/tranquille/chère/bon marché.

May I please have a pillow? *Je voudrais un oreiller, s'il vous plaît.*

May I leave my children/wife/husband with the concierge?
Pourrais-je laisser mes enfants / ma femme/mon mari avec le concierge?

I can't open the window. *Je n'arrive pas à ouvrir la fenêtre.*

Where can I get some fresh air? *Où peut-on trouver un peu d'air?*

May I have a room over the garden/courtyard?
Je voudrais une chambre sur le jardin/la cour.

Get out of my room! *Sortez de ma chambre!*

Leave me alone! *Laissez-moi tranquille!*

Is this really tea? *C'est vraiment du thé ça?*

The shower/bath/loo is blocked.
La douche/la baignoire/le wc est bouché.

My wallet/key/baby is locked in the cupboard.
J'ai enfermé mon porte-monnaie/ma clé/mon bébé dans l'armoire.

How old is this bread? *De quand date ce pain?*

My bed sags/is hard/soft. *Mon lit est défoncé/trop dur/trop mou*

The cold water is hot. *L'eau froide est chaude.*

I've scalded the baby. *J'ai échaudé le bébé.*

Call a doctor please. *Appelez un médicin s'il vous plaît.*

There is no plug for the basin/bath.
Il n'y a pas de bouchon pour le lavabo/la baignoire.

Please remove that spider. *Enlevez cette araignée, s'il vous plaît.*

MAKING THE MOST OF PARIS

When you are in museum mood

Museum visits are made easy with the *Carte Musées et Monuments*, a pass valid in over 60 museums and worth buying if you are planning to make your visit intensely cultural. Available at museums, big Metro and RER stations and the Tourist Office, 127 avenue des Champs Élysées.

The Louvre is half price after 3pm, free the first Sunday in the month. A queue-beating tip when the line at the pyramid looks 24 hours long – on foot, face the Tuileries, your back to the pyramid: to your left and right, next to the angels, are stairs to the underground entrance. By metro, get off at the *Palais Royal-Musée du Louvre* station and use the entrance signposted directly from the platform.

When you have museum indigestion

General tip: FUSAC is a free, fortnightly English-language magazine full of useful stuff for all Anglo-Parisians on where to find community events, like-minded people, nannies, house-moving sales, etc. Can be found in the English-language bookshops and in bars, sandwich shops, etc in trendy areas.

Cinemas

Cinema programmes go from Wednesday to Tuesday: the week's listings come out on the Tuesday before the new programme starts.

Information: Two publications, both in French: *L'Officiel des Spectacles*, which costs the princely sum of 35cts, and *Pariscope* which also lists film festival programmes and unsavoury advertisements for expensive telephone conversations and therefore costs 40cts. Both carry information on theatres, exhibitions, concerts, cinemas, restaurants, nightclubs, etc.

Language: We all know that a large proportion of films are in English so, if you want to see one of the latest productions or catch up on a golden oldie, lash out on a programme and plan a different kind of culture trip. NB *Version originale* (vo) means 'original language' with French subtitles; *version française* (vf) means dubbed in French.

Which cinema? On any day of the year there are some 150 different films showing in the city and most central Paris cinemas systematically show films in their 'original language'. A few can be relied on to have good undubbed films; most are in the 5th and 6th arrondissements.

And there is one small, private 'chain' called MK2, owned by maverick distributor Marin Karmitz whose avowed aim is to remain independent from the big American cowboys and to promote good films rather than commercial blockbusters. A man to be encouraged.

IMPORTANT In some cases, you are still expected to tip the usherette – a modest 40cts or so will do. If this annoys you, just remember that this may be her only income.

Bookshops Books are more expensive in France than in England, not because bookshops are greedier but because books bear higher sales tax.

English language bookshops

Shakespeare & Co, 37 rue de la Bûcherie, Paris 5th. Metro: Maubert-Mutualité. Old secondhand bookshop on several floors: books on the floor, squeezed into every staircase, more bookcases than walking space on the upper floors – irresistible. It is a long-standing Franco-American institution where Great Names We Have Nurtured – James Joyce in particular – are standard currency and the owner George Whitman still holds Sunday afternoon tea parties and poetry readings. Mostly staffed by friendly American students.

WH Smith, 248 rue de Rivoli, Paris 1st. Metro: Concorde. Yes, there is a Paris branch, refreshingly different and independent of the mother house, carrying a large number of books currently in print in Britain and America. Efficient, bilingual, mainly French staff.

Galignani, 224 rue de Rivoli, Paris 1st. Metro: Concorde. "The first English bookshop on the Continent." A very smart Franco-Anglo-American bookshop with old fashioned panelling and a superior atmosphere. Lots of art books, literature and browsing material as well as normal holiday books. Bilingual staff of both nationalities.

Brentano's, 37 avenue de l'Opéra, Paris 2nd. Metro: Opéra. Big American bookshop: endless corridors and corners with masses of books, magazines, all kinds of upbeat stationery. A must for many. I once saw a Rolls Royce + chauffeur park on the pavement and release two fearfully smart, diminutive women who marched into the emporium of culture with their enormous, gorilla-like bodyguard, at their heels. The staff were just as friendly with him as they are with all clients.

Tea & Tattered Pages, 24 rue Mayet, Paris 6th. Metro: Duroc. This is, as its name suggests, a teashop which also sells secondhand books. A supremely friendly, student-like atmosphere in a small shop where people come to read (even buy) books and sit chatting for hours.

The Red Wheelbarrow Bookstore, 13 rue Charles V, Paris 4th. Metro: Sully-Morland. The shop is run by 3 Americans but they stock English and American literature, history of Paris and France, translations into English of good French books, lots of children's books and… there's a piano in the shop. They do readings too.

French bookshops

A few are worth mentioning for their wide variety or narrow speciality.

FNAC. Metro: Étoile, Forum des Halles, Saint Lazare, Montparnasse. The French answer to Smiths, Dillons, Waterstones and Menzies all rolled into one. There are several branches in Paris (and in large provincial towns), with big selections on all general subjects and usually an English-language section.

Gibert Jeune and Joseph Gibert, Place St Michel. Metro: St Michel. Facing each other and run by estranged members of the same family, they are a sort of French Foyles who also sell stationery, records and secondhand textbooks. Much frequented by the student population.

La Hune, 170 boulevard Saint Germain, Paris 6th. Metro: St Michel. A lively place just next to the Café de Flore, it stays open late in the evening and has very good art and literature sections.

La Procure, 3 rue Mézières, Paris 6th. Metro: St Sulpice. Specialises in religion but has excellent philosophy and fiction sections too. Much used by philosophy teachers and students.

La Méridienne, 14 rue du Dragon, Paris 6th. Metro: St Germain des Prés. In a delightful courtyard, it sells books on therapy, spirituality and modern self-development.

La Maison du Dictionnaire, 98 boulevard du Montparnasse, Paris 14th. Metro: Montparnasse. Astounding! Nothing but dictionaries – languages, of course, even the most obscure; and all manner of technical, mechanical and electronical spheres.

Markets Visit the food markets of Paris, soak up the feel of daily life here, even buy some of the ingredients that make it what it is. Covered markets may be in superb 19th-century iron-and-glass buildings. Some street markets consist of temporary stands set up two or three days a week, others are pedestrian streets where the permanent shops simply extend their space onto the pavements. They are always colourful, lively and full of temptations (plus a few pickpockets) among their amazingly-crafted mountains of fruit and vegetables. The stall-holders are unlikely to be locals – more probably from the suburbs, North Africa or Turkey, their styles in interesting contrast with those of their clients. The last half hour before closing time on Sundays – midday or 1pm – can be rich in unrefusable 'finishing up' offers.

Look for fruit and veg stalls saying *maraicher*. They are market gardeners bringing good food direct from producer to end user.

Covered Markets

Marché Saint Germain, 6th. Metro: Saint Germain des Prés. Expensive but very good on fish and fresh vegetables. Also an excellent Greek stall with delicious picnic ingredients.

Marché Saint Quentin, 10th, Metro: Gare de l'Est. This magnificent 19th-century iron polygon has a variety of stalls including Portuguese, Italian and Kosher specialities, hardware and cobbling shops, excellent cheese, vegetable, fish and *charcuterie* and a café in the middle!

Rue du Château, 10th. Metro: Château d'Eau. Organic Market: all day, Tuesday-Sunday. The only permanent, covered organic market in Paris, it's wonderful. (Organic = *Produits Biologique*.)

Street Markets (every day except Mondays)

Place d'Aligre, 11th. Metro: Ledru-Rollin. Cheapest of 'em all, but make sure of the quality before you buy. Tremendous atmosphere in the crush of eager shoppers, North African voices and spicy smells. The covered market has better stuff – at higher prices. Plus a tempting section dealing in junk, secondhand clothes and crockery on weekday mornings.

Rue Mouffetard, 5th. Metro: Monge. Super little market at the bottom of the hill on place Saint Médard, and yet more tempting stands, shops and eating places as you walk up towards the Place de la Contrescarpe and the historic centre of the Latin Quarter.

Rue Cler, 7th. Metro: Latour Maubourg. Nicely crowded and bustly and human in a fairly smart, superior neighbourhood.

Rue de Lévis, 17th. Metro: Villiers. A car-empty, market-filled street where people take time to pick and choose and to talk to each other.

Occasional Street Markets

Open mornings only (8am-1pm), they are often cheaper and simpler than the daily markets. The best are probably:

Bd de Port-Royal, Paris 5th. Metro: Gobelins. Tuesday, Thursday, Saturday.

Bd Auguste Blanqui, Paris 13th. Metro: Corvisart. Tuesday, Friday, Saturday.

Bd Edgar Quinet, Paris 14th. Metro: Edgar Quinet. Wednesday, Saturday.

Bd Richard Lenoir, Paris 11th. Metro: Bastille. Thursday, Sunday.

Organic

And, although most of the others have one organic/health-food stall, there are two wholly organic weekly markets (*marchés biologiques*) that are worth a visit if you care about natural food, soap, cosmetics, etc.

Saturday mornings Bd des Batignolles, Paris 17th.
Metro: Rome.

Sunday mornings Bd Raspail, Paris 6th.
Metro: Sèvres-Babylone.

Fabrics

Cleaning ladies and countesses will go all the way to Montmartre to buy the fabrics and accessories they need for their dressmaking or interior decoration projects. The Marché Saint Pierre, a series of shops in the little streets at the bottom of the Square Willette which itself sits beneath the Sacré Coeur, is a Parisian institution. Here, especially at the house of Dreyfus, they know they will find a wide choice of reasonably-priced materials (the wealthy

MAKING THE MOST OF PARIS

Dreyfus family are more likely to be found frequenting their countess clients than their cleaning ladies).

Stamps and Phonecards

The long-standing stamp collectors' exchange market on the pavement benches on Avenue Matignon, just off the Rond-Point des Champs Élysées, now deals in phonecards as well. All day Thursday, Saturday, Sunday.

Gardens The public 'green spaces' (*espaces verts*) of Paris are few and far between, which makes them very precious. Most are rather formally French with a small piece called *le jardin anglais* where things are meant to look more spontaneous and 'wild'. More and more municipal gardeners are sowing tough grass seed so that at last the French may be allowed to walk and sit on the grass in their public gardens; a few still hold dear the old interdiction and employ whistlers to keep order.

Visits

Paris City Hall organises excellent guided visits of Paris parks and gardens: see announcement at the back of this book.

Fête des Jardins. On one weekend a year, over 100 gardens, large and small, that are otherwise closed to the public are visible – the difficulty is choosing which ones to visit in the short space of time. 3rd weekend in September. Contact: local Mairies.

On the Edge

The two biggest 'green areas' are outside Paris proper: the Bois de Boulogne on the western front, the Bois de Vincennes to the east. Both have lakes where you can go rowing, both have roads through them but still manage to grow more trees and grass than the rest of our parks put together. Definitely the smaller, Boulogne has a couple of famous race courses (Longchamp & Auteuil) and an 'amusement park' (*Jardin d'Acclimatation*), a deliciously old-fashioned hangover from gentler days where modern French children still seem happy with swings and slides and the little zoo. Vincennes, which also has a race course, is more of a people's park and has a wonderful old 17th-century fort.

MAKING THE MOST OF PARIS

Inside the Walls (Paris intramuros = the 20 arrondissements)

Inside Paris, the Jardin du Luxembourg is still a favourite
with the solid old Senate building (Palais du Luxembourg)
as its backdrop. There is enormous character in its declarative
19th-century statues, studied French formality and very staid,
definitely pre-90s amusements for children that come in
the form of really slow pony rides and model-yacht-sailing
on the pond (boats for hire on the spot – NO motors). The
old *chaisières* – chair ladies – tyrants who used to come round
demanding a few centimes for the chair you had chosen to sit
on, have gone; but the population is still an interesting mixture
of Left Bank *grand-mères* and Sorbonne students.

The next slot goes to the newest garden in Paris, the Parc
André Citroën, way down the river beyond the Eiffel Tower.
Built on the site of the old car factories, it is a brilliant study in
modern public park design: two very daring greenhouses and
several smaller ones, all built with what look like smoothed-
down tree trunks, a series of colour gardens, fascinating
waterworks and a balanced mix of open space and secluded
corners. They have even created an overgrown, weedy, 'bomb-
site' area. Well worth the trip.

Behind the Eiffel Tower, the Champ de Mars was laid out at
the end of the 18th century as the practice ground for students
at the *École Militaire*: it has some nice spots with benches (and
uniforms with whistles to shoo you off the grass). Out in the
19th arrondissement, the magnificent Buttes Chaumont (*monts
chauves* or bald hills) is a series of steep hills (windmills used to
stand here) and a reproduction of the Sibyl's Temple – deliciously
19th century.

Two lesser parks: the Parc Montsouris, on the southern edge
of Paris, is hilly and green and natural-looking and, in the
smart residential neighbourhood north of the Champs Elysées,
the Parc Monceau (another bald hill) still has the aristocratic
bearing of its origins (it was built in 1780 as the private garden
for the Duke of Chartres' country cottage).

And there are hidden green treasures behind high walls, in
ministry and hospital grounds. Not all are open to the public
but you risk no more than a stiff watchdog's bark if you stick
your nose in where you're not wanted, so do try. The gardens

of the Hôpital La Pitié/Salpêtrière are a wonderful surprise
– and their chapel is almost the size of a small cathedral. The
Hôpital Saint Louis has unexpected peace round the lawns and
flowerbeds of its ancient courtyards. Built in the same style and
by the same architect as the brick-and-stone Place des Vosges,
it is also an architectural curiosity (there's a lot of modern
hospital in the grounds now, too). The garden of the Rodin
Museum (accessible if you buy a museum ticket) makes a
visit there even more rewarding and the Palais Royal enfolds
a delightful leafy and airy space within its stone embrace. In
the Square Catherine Laboure (Rue de Babylone) is a real
and beautifully kept kitchen garden while on the roof of the
Gare Montparnasse is a huge surprise: the Jardin Atlantique,
a diminutive 'ocean-view park' with trees, paths, corners
and vistas.

Les Serres d'Auteuil are owned by the city and their lovely
19th-century glasshouses are really worth a visit. They grow
seedlings for the public parks and gardens, though the palm
trees and Japanese carp just live their lives out here.

Last, as in every great city, the cemeteries (*cimetières*) are places
of vegetation, stone and eternal rest and some people enjoy
the search for memorials to Great Heroes (or pop singers,
or politicians). Montparnasse on the Left Bank, Père Lachaise
on the Right Bank are the best known but Montmartre also
has some interesting tombs on its hillside.

How to get there

Jardin d'Acclimatation/Bois de Boulogne Metro: Porte Maillot,
Sablons. Bois de Vincennes Metro: Château de Vincennes. Jardin
du Luxembourg Metro: Odéon. Champ de Mars Metro: École
Militaire. Buttes Chaumont Metro: Buttes Chaumont. Parc
Montsouris Metro: Cité Universitaire. Parc Monceau Metro:
Monceau. Hôpital La Pitié/Salpêtrière Metro: St Marcel. Hôpital
St Louis Metro: Goncourt. Musée Rodin Metro: Varenne. Palais
Royal Metro: Palais Royal. Cimetière Montparnasse Metro:
Edgar Quinet. Cimetière Père Lachaise Metro: Père Lachaise.
Cimetière de Montmartre Metro: La Fourche.

Walks   The River Seine is the city's largest lung but walking along it
was made difficult in the 1990s when the authorities decided
they had to offer as much space as possible to King Car. Ideas

are changing and some of those fume-filled ways are being
returned to the humble pedestrian and his dog.

The plan is to provide unbroken pathways and footbridges
from the Parc de Bercy in the east right round to the Parc
André Citroën in the west – a 12-kilometre dream of which
a chunk in the east has already come true.

The two islands: Cité and Saint Louis are good wandering areas,
apart from the main north-south link between Châtelet and
St Michel. Guided walks, in French or English, are listed
every week in *L'Officiel des Spectacles* and *Pariscope*. Here are
a very few suggestions from us.

1. See the new permanent open-air sculpture garden along the
river west of the Gare d'Austerlitz below Quai Saint Bernard.
On summer evenings, each little riverside bay of this garden
is given over to a type of music or dance: drumming displays,
tango, country dancing, many more - come and join in.

At the end, cross over to Ile Saint Louis and walk along by those
elegant 17th-century apartment buildings, built for the high-
born and wealthy of their day and still very select places to
live. Take the Pont Saint Louis across to the Ile de la Cité and
the little garden below the east end of Notre Dame – don't
miss the memorial to the Jewish deportees at the very eastern
point of the garden.

Walk west along the cathedral, gazing up at the stone miracles
overhead, across the square past the hospital that is still known
by its medieval name of God's Hostel (Hôtel Dieu) and right for
a brief spell in all that traffic until you reach the Flower Market
which feels like a slice of tropical jungle adrift in northern
Europe. And here is the Cité metro station with its original
Guimard entrance, whence you can go north or south as you
wish.

2. As well as its world famous examples of national building
styles, built between the 1920s and the 1950s to house foreign
and French students in an ideal of harmony and international
understanding, the Cité Universitaire is in fact a vast 40-hectare
park, so visitors can combine culture AND fresh(er) air.

3. Wandering perpendicular to the Seine (one stretch is in a
tunnel), the deliciously immobile, old-fashioned Canal Saint

Martin was condemned to death by concrete in the 1970s but good sense prevailed. It is a stretch of tree-lined water where working and pleasure barges climb up and down the nine locks, Sunday afternoons are no-traffic times on the roads alongside and walking northwards is most enjoyable, ending with the treat of a good MK2 cinema (cf. § Cinemas) and café on the banks of the Bassin de la Villette. Canal trips inside Paris or out into the countryside along the River Marne or the Canal de l'Ourcq are organised by Canauxrama, based at Bassin de la Villette.

4. A new walkway now occupies the old railway line between Bastille (just SE of) and Daumesnil. Called the Coulée Verte (the Green Stream), it is effectively a long thin line that has been equipped with trees and bushes, benches and entrance staircases and runs all the way at 2nd-floor level above the road. A most original addition to the grass-starved Paris and when you have had enough of walking in a straight line you can take the stairs down and visit the craftsmen working and selling their wares underneath the arches.

High Places Apart from the inevitable Eiffel Tower (the highest spot at 276 metres but it costs a lot to get to the top), you can climb the steps to the top of the towers of Notre Dame (69m) for an incomparable view over the heart of medieval Paris and a study of the architecture of the cathedral itself. The department store La Samaritaine, at Châtelet, has lifts to its top floor, a café on the roof terrace and charges nothing for this bird's-eye view of the very centre of Paris (46m). The Tour Montparnasse is the second highest viewing point (209m) and has "the fastest lifts in Europe" to its 52nd floor: go up to the bar, order a drink – and get the view with it.

Cookery Demonstrations Cookery demonstrations by Cordon Bleu chefs on weekdays lasting 2-3 hours, maybe given in, or translated into English and end with a tasting. Price € 38. Book 48hrs ahead on 01 53 68 22 50.

Getting Around Paris The layout. Finding your way in Paris is easier if you know that-

1. The city is divided into 20 arrondissements laid out in a clockwise spiral pattern that starts at Place de la Concorde.

2. Street numbering is based on the Seine, i.e. streets perpendicular to the river are numbered outwards from it, odds on the left, evens on the right; streets parallel to the river are numbered as the river flows, east to west.

3. The Left Bank (*rive gauche*) is the south bank, the Right Bank (*rive droite*) is the north bank of the River Seine.

The maps in this guide are not street maps. Bring or buy one of the Indispendable™, Taride™, Michelin or other pocket street atlases and get the excellent map of metro and bus lines free from any metro station.

DON'T use your car. It will cost you a fortune in parking or pound fees and in frustration looking for somewhere to leave it. Also, Paris is already dangerously polluted and no-one needs to add to that.

DO use the wonderful public transport system, run by the RATP. It is one of the best in the world. Some bus routes are perfect tours of Paris and its monuments.

Buses

The No 24 crosses the Seine twice and runs along the south embankment between the bridges. Other good routes are 30, 48, 73, 82 and 90. Left-bank route 88, the first new bus line in 50 years, opened in 1998 between the Cité Universitaire and the Parc André Citroën, takes you past Montparnasse and the postmodern architecture of the Place de Catalogne, then on through the residential 15th arrondissement to the high-rise buildings of the new Left Bank development called Front de Seine.

Metro

You are never far from one of the 300-odd metro stations and trains run between 5.30am and about 1am. Many of the stations have been radically refurbished in the last few years, especially for the metro's 100th anniversary in 2000, and are full of interest just for themselves. The new line 14 is a showcase for the latest thing in driverless trains and is designed to take some of the load off the other Right-Bank lines between the great new Bibliothèque François Mitterand and the Madeleine.

Tickets

Fares are paid according to the number of zones crossed. Visitors will normally not go outside zones 1 and 2, the city limits. One ticket is valid for one journey by bus, metro or RER within zones 1 and 2. You should keep your ticket for inspection at any time and for the turnstiles OUT of RER systems.

Single ticket € 1.30, a book of 10 tickets € 9.60.

A one-day *Mobilis* ticket for two zones : € 5.

A two-zone pass – *Carte Orange* – for unlimited travel by the holder (passport photo required) within the two zones for one week: € 13.75 per person; for one month: € 46.05 per person.

Other formulas for one to five days exist to cover more zones (*Paris Visite*) or to include museum entrance (*Carte Musée*).

Batobus

Not the speediest way to travel but great fun with lots to see, the boatbus uses the great watery road through the middle of Paris to take you, in six stops, from the Eiffel Tower to the Hôtel de Ville.

Bicycles

You can hire a bike and launch yourself bravely into the scrum alone or you can take a guided bike tour, in French or English, from

Paris-Vélo, 2 rue du Fer-à-Moulin, 5th. Tel: 01 43 37 59 22. Paris à Vélo c'est Sympa, 37 bd Bourdon, 4th. Tel: 01 48 87 60 01, have bikes for hire – folding bikes, tandems, baby seats – and organise little tours.

Roue Libre, passage Mondétour, 75001. Tel: 0810 44 15 34. Bikes for hire for weekends and national holidays, March-Oct.

Roller Skate and Roller Blades

If you want a direct experience of what lively outdoor Paris is doing today, go to Nomades, 37 bd Bourdon, 4th. Tel: 01 44 54 07 44. The place hums with everything you ever wanted to own, hire or learn about *les rollers*:

- Roller skates and blades for hire at € 8 per day, € 1 for the armour-plating

- Lessons on the country's biggest indoor roller-floor (in the suburbs).

- Sunday afternoon roller-treks for all the family from their front door. These draw thousands of enthusiasts and are free. (The equally popular Friday evening outing starts from Montparnasse at 22h.)

- Roller tours of Paris - five different cultural themes.

MAKING THE MOST OF PARIS

Roller Station, 107 boulevard Beaumarchais, 3rd,
Tel: 01 42 78 33 00, also hire out roller skates and blades.

Airport Buses

Orlybus between Orly Airport and Place Denfert-Rochereau,
Paris 14th.

Roissybus between Charles-de-Gaulle Airport and Opéra,
Paris 9th.

Air France buses between:

Charles-de-Gaulle Airport and Étoile or Porte Maillot or
Montparnasse;

Orly Airport and Invalides or Montparnasse.

Airport Shuttle: private door-to-door minibus service at
reasonable prices. Some hotels subscribe. Tel: 01 45 38 55 72.

Dates to Remember

Late Feb-early March: Salon de l'Agriculture Porte de
Versailles, 15th. Metro: Porte de Versailles. "The biggest farm
in Europe" when the countryside comes to the capital, bringing
its finest bulls, ewes and carrots in a joyful atmosphere of
Crufts-for-Cows; also some wonderful opportunities to
sample fine regional cooking.

Mid-March: Le Printemps des Rues Between République,
Bastille and Nation, hundreds of street entertainers.

April-May: La Foire du Trône Pelouse de Reuilly, 12th. Metro:
Porte Dorée. A gigantic funfair where the families and youth
of Paris and the suburbs flock for ghost trains, roundabouts
and candyfloss.

Good Friday: Le Chemin de Croix, Montmatre Square Willette,
18th. Metro: Anvers. The Archbishop of Paris walks the stations
of the cross on the way up to Sacré Coeur.

End June: La Course des Garçons de Café A supremely Parisian
race where hundreds of waiters and waitresses in full regalia –
black suit, white apron, glasses on tray – run a crazy distance
(those who finish have done 5 miles) along the boulevards with
those glasses on that tray.

MAKING THE MOST OF PARIS

13th and 14th July: Bastille Day The famous bals populaires (dancing in the street) take place the evening before the day itself. Parisians dance on the bones of the Bastille prison, of course, and also at fire stations: the bals des pompiers are much favoured. On the official day, the 14th: military parade on the Champs Élysées in the morning, city fireworks over the Trocadéro.

3rd weekend in September: All over town. Programme from Tourist Office or Mairies (cf. Gardens above).

1st weekend in October: Montmartre wine harvest. More festivities than wine: the event, full of fun and pseudo-traditional ritual, is far bigger than the harvest from this tiny vineyard. The wine, pressed in the Mairie itself, is expensive for what it is... but so exclusive.

2nd weekend in November: Marjolaine Green Lifestyle exhibition Parc Floral de Paris, 12th. Metro: Château de Vincennes. Stands and stalls, lectures and lessons – everyone in the green, organic, environmental and alternative health world comes to see and be seen; new and interesting products and ideas are launched here every year.

FRENCH PERIOD FURNITURE

To enliven your reading of the entries in this book and perhaps illumine your stay in the hotels listed, here is a very brief history of French furniture in the 17th, 18th and 19th centuries with the essential features of each style, an illustration by Mathias Fournier and the dates of the king or government associated with the name (the period often covers more time than the actual reign).

Louis XIII 1610-1643

Solid, square and massive are the key characteristics here. Twists and turns, carvings and heavy ornamentation with 'grotesque' masks, figurines and cherubs, garlands, bunches of fruit and scrollwork to decorate the dark wood of the structure.

Louis XIV 1643-1715

Louis was five when he came to the throne and reigned in person from 1661. Luxurious and elaborate describe his period and Boulle, founder of his own style and first in a line of craftsmen, was the leading designer and cabinet-maker. He launched the fashion for using expensive foreign woods plus tortoishell, ivory and brass as inlay; gilt bronze for corner trim, handles and finger-plate decoration; deeply carved garlands, festoons, allegorical motifs and mythological figures to celebrate the power and wealth of the régime, elaborate curves to counteract the solid squareness of earlier times.

Régence 1715–1723*

Reaction to the excesses of Louis' court lifestyle set in before he died. The need was for quieter, more informal surroundings. Furniture became lighter, less elaborately adorned, more gently shaped. Heavy, deepset carvings and bronze bits were replaced by flat curves and flowing ribbons. Life, manners and art became less declamatory, less pompous, more delicate.

*Almost a century before the English Regency period.

Louis XV 1715–1771

Another child king, he reigned in person after 1723. The Régence search for more delicacy led, under Louis XV, into the Rococo style and the craze for all things oriental - Chinoiscrie was IN with its lacquer, ivory and mother-of-pearl inlays and lively, exotic scenes of faraway places. Comfort was important too, with fine fabrics and well-padded chairs. So was beautiful handiwork: the period produced some superb craftsmen.

FRENCH PERIOD FURNITURE

Louis XVI 1774-1793

Instantly recognisable by its tapering fluted legs and straight lines, this is the style associated with Marie-Antoinette and the yearning of sophisticated urbanites for a simpler Golden Age when the countryside was the source of all Good, though few actually made the transition. Furniture was often painted in 'rustic' pastel colours, and marquetry was still widely used for more formal pieces. The simplicity of classical forms was the model, inspired by numerous archaeological expeditions.

Directoire 1795-1799

This is when women started to dress like Greek goddesses and gentlemen wore long flowing coats and high boots. Furniture design continued the trend towards simple flowing lines, less decoration and ever more reference to ancient Rome (Pompeii revealed its treasure at this time, to everyone's great excitement). There is a derived Swedish style called Gustavian.

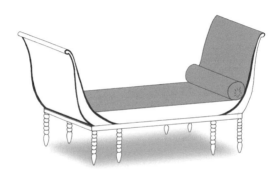

FRENCH PERIOD FURNITURE

Empire 1704–1815

The Emperor was Napoleon I, the inspiration
was his booty from the Egyptian campaigns
– as well as more Ancient Greece and Rome.
Ormolu ornamentation took the form of
sphinxes' busts, winged lions and forms were
even direct copies from Antiquity. Later, the
trend was to over-elaboration and a certain
type of decadence.

Fauteuil Voltaire 1850s

With or without arms, usually dressed in
tapestry-style weave or deep-coloured plush
and shiny studs, this is a ubiquitous item in
French houses, hotels and inns. Voltaire,
philosopher of religious, political and social
liberty and recognised figurehead of the
18th-century Enlightenment, died in 1778.
His portraits often show him wearing a soft
velvety coat and floppy lace trimmings. The
chair that bears his name is in fact a mid-
19th-century invention but it matches the
popular image of Voltaire and one can well
imagine the great man reclining in his lace
cuffs and addressing a group of literary
ladies in a smart salon.

Napoleon III 1852–1870

This period, also known as Second Empire,
just to confuse you, or the Beaux-Arts style,
was the French equivalent of heavy Victorian.
Thick velvet drapes hung everywhere, tassels,
swags, fringes adorned them, keeping the
light out; the classical style became massive
and was decorated with pints of gilding; it
used rich dark colours, heavy dark woods,
much gilt bronze ornamentation (e.g. little
balconies round little occasional tables,
elaborate light fittings), veined marble tops
on storage pieces, and cover-ups for all legs
or "understandings."

WHAT IS ALASTAIR SAWDAY PUBLISHING?

Fifteen or more of us work in converted barns on a farm near Bristol, close enough to the city for a bicycle ride and far enough for a silence broken only by horses and the occasional passage of a tractor. Some editors work in the countries they write about, e.g. France; others work from the UK but are based outside the office. We enjoy each other's company, celebrate every event possible, and work in an easy-going but committed environment.

These books owe their style and mood to Alastair's miscellaneous career and his interest in the community and the environment. He has taught overseas, worked with refugees, run development projects abroad, founded a travel company and several environmental organisations. There has been a slightly mad streak evident throughout, not least in his driving of a waste-paper-collection lorry for a year, the manning of stalls at jumble sales and the pursuit of causes long before they were considered sane.

These books owe their style and mood to Alastair's miscellaneous career and his interest in the community and the environment

Back to the travel company: trying to take his clients to eat and sleep in places that were not owned by corporations and assorted bandits he found dozens of very special places in France – farms, châteaux etc – a list that grew into the first book, French Bed and Breakfast. It was a celebration of 'real' places to stay and the remarkable people who run them.

The publishing company grew from that first and rather whimsical French book. It started as a mild crusade, and there it stays – full of 'attitude', and the more appealing for it. For we still celebrate the unusual, the beautiful, the individual. We are passionate about rejecting the banal, the ugly, the pompous and the indifferent and we are passionate too about 'real' food. Alastair is a trustee of the Soil Association and keen to promote organic growing and consuming by owners and visitors.

It is a source of deep pleasure to us to know that there are many thousands of people who share our views. We are by no means alone in trumpeting the virtues of resisting the destruction and uniformity of so much of our culture and the cultures of other nations, too.

We run a company in which people and values matter. We love to hear of new friendships between those in the book and those using it, and to know that there are many people – among them farmers – who have been enabled to pursue their decent lives thanks to the extra income our books bring them.

WWW.SPECIALPLACESTOSTAY.COM

Britain

France

Ireland

Italy

Portugal

Spain...

all in one place!

On the unfathomable and often unnavigable sea of internet accommodation pages, those who have discovered **www.specialplacestostay.com** have found it to be an island of reliability. Not only will you find a database full of honest, trustworthy, up to date information about all our Special Places to Stay across Europe, but also:

- Links to the web sites of well over a thousand places from the series
- Colourful, clickable, interactive maps to help you find the right place
- The facility to make most bookings by e-mail – even if you don't have e-mail yourself
- Online purchasing of our books, securely and cheaply
- Regular, exclusive special offers on titles from the series
- The latest news about future editions, new titles and new places
- The chance to participate in the evolution of the site and the books

The site is constantly evolving and is frequently updated. We've revised our maps, adding more useful and interesting links, providing news, updates and special features that won't appear anywhere else but in our window on the worldwide web.

Just as with our printed guides, your feedback counts, so when you've surfed all this and you still want more, let us know – this site has been planted with room to grow.

Russell Wilkinson, Web Producer
website@specialplacestostay.com

If you'd like to receive news and updates about our books by e-mail, send a message to newsletter@specialplacestostay.com

ALASTAIR SAWDAY'S

**British Hotels, Inns &
Other Places**
Edition 4   £12.99

British Bed & Breakfast
Edition 7   £14.99

British Holiday Homes
Edition 1   £x.xx

Garden Bed & Breakfast
Edition 2   £14.99

French Bed & Breakfast
Edition 8   £15.99

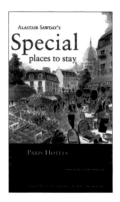

Paris Hotels
Edition 4   £9.99

**French Hotels, Inns &
Other Places**
Edition 2   £11.95

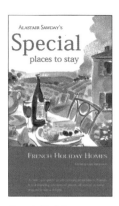

French Holiday Homes
Edition 1   £11.99

London
Edition 1   £9.99

SPECIAL PLACES TO STAY SERIES

Spain
Edition 4   £11.95

Italy
Edition 2   £11.95

Ireland
Edition 3   £10.95

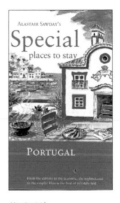

Portugal
Edition 1   £8.95

THE LITTLE EARTH BOOK

Over 30,000 copies sold.

A fascinating read. The earth is now desperately vulnerable; so are we. Original, stimulating short essays about what is going wrong with our planet, and about the greatest challenge of our century: how to save the Earth for us all. It is succinct, yet intellectually credible, well-referenced, wry yet deadly serious.

Researched and written by a Bristol architect, James Bruges, The Little Earth Book is a clarion call to action, a stimulating collection of short essays on today's most important environmental concerns, from global warming and poisoned food to unfettered economic growth, Third World debt, genes and 'superbugs'. Undogmatic but sure-footed, the style is light, explaining complex issues with easy language, illustrations and cartoons. Ideas are developed chapter by chapter, yet each one stands alone. It is an easy browse.

The Little Earth Book provides hope, with new ideas and examples of people swimming against the current, for bold ideas that work in practice. It is a book as important as it is original. Learn about the issues and join the most important debate of this century.

Did you know?

- If everyone adopted the Western lifestyle we would need five earths to support us.
- In 50 years the US has — with intensive pesticide use — doubled the amount of crops lost to pests.
- Environmental disasters have already created more than 80 MILLION refugees.

www.littleearth.co.uk

And now The Little Food Book! Same style, same purpose: it blows the lid off the food 'industry' — in a concise, entertaining way. It is pithy, deeply informative and an important contribution to the great food debate…

THE LITTLE FOOD BOOK

Our own livelihoods are at risk – from the food we eat. Original, stimulating, mini-essays about what is wrong with our food today, and about the greatest challenge of the new century: how to produce enough food without further damaging our health, the environment and vulnerable countries.

Written by Craig Sams, Chairman of the Soil Association, it is concise, deeply informative and an important contribution to the great food debate. Just like The Little Earth Book, this is pithy, yet intellectually credible, wry yet deadly serious.

- A brilliant and easy-to-read synthesis of complex subjects
- Pertinent   food is a daily issue – organics, Genetically-Modified crops, farming practices, healthy eating
- Especially timely – the decline of the rural economy, foot and mouth, changes to the Commom Agricultural Policy
- Compact size – an excellent Christmas present or stocking filler.

Extracts from book:
- "In the UK alone 25,000,000 kilos of pesticides are sprayed on food every year."
- "In 2001 the World Trade Organisation fined the EU $120 million for suggesting that US meat imports should label the presence of hormone residues."
- "Aspartame is a neurotoxin that probably causes as much brain damage as mobile phone use."
- "300,000 Americans a year die of obesity."
- "Research indicates that monosodiumglutamate is a contributing factor in Alzheimer's disease."
- "Globally, the market for organic food in 2001 exceeded $20 billion."

There is room for optimism – but you need to read this engrossing little book first!

REPORT FORM

Comments on existing entries and new discoveries

If you have any comments on entries in this guide, please let us have them. If you have a favourite house, hotel, inn or other new discovery, not just in Paris, please let us know about it.

Book title: _____

Entry no: _____ Edition no: _____

New recommendation: _____

Country: _____

Name of property: _____

Address: _____

_____

_____

Postcode: _____

Tel: _____

Date of stay: _____

Comments: _____

_____

_____

From: _____

Address: _____

_____

_____

Postcode: _____

Tel: _____

Please send the completed form to:

Alastair Sawday Publishing,
The Home Farm Stables, Barrow Gurney, Bristol BS48 3RW
or go to www.specialplacestostay.com and click on 'contact'.

Thank you.

ORDER FORM UK

All these Special Places to Stay books and The Little Earth Book and The Little Food Book are available in major bookshops or you may order them direct. Post and packaging are FREE.

		Price	No. copies
French Bed & Breakfast	Edition 8	£15.99	
French Hotels, Inns and other places	Edition 2	£11.99	
French Holiday Homes	Edition 1	£11.99	
Paris Hotels	Edition 4	£9.99	
British Bed & Breakfast	Edition 7	£14.99	
British Hotels, Inns and other places	Edition 4	£12.99	
Garden Bed & Breakfast	Edition 1	£10.95	
London	Edition 1	£9.99	
Ireland	Edition 3	£10.95	
Spain	Edition 4	£11.95	
Portugal	Edition 3	£0.95	
Italy	Edition 2	£11.95	
The Little Earth Book	Edition 3	£6.99	
The Little Food Book	Edition 1	£6.99	
	Total £		

Please make cheques payable to **Alastair Sawday Publishing**

Please send cheques to: Alastair Sawday Publishing, The Home Farm Stables, Barrow Gurney, Bristol BS48 3RW. For credit card orders call 01275 464891 or order directly from our website **www.specialplacestostay.com**

Title _____ First name _____

Surname _____

Address _____

_____

_____

Postcode _____

Tel _____

If you do not wish to receive mail from other like-minded companies, please tick here ☐

If you would prefer not to receive information about special offers on our books, please tick here ☐

PH4

ORDER FORM USA

All these books are available at your local bookstore, or you may order direct. Allow two to three weeks for delivery.

		Price	No. copies
Portugal	Edition 1	$14.95	
Spain	Edition 4	$19.95	
Ireland	Edition 3	$17.95	
Paris Hotels	Edition 3	$14.95	
Garden Bed & Breakfast	Edition 1	$17.95	
British Hotels, Inns and other places	Edition 4	$17.95	
French Hotels, Inns and other places	Edition 2	$19.95	
British Bed & Breakfast	Edition 7	$19.95	
London	Edition 1	$12.95	
Italy	Edition 2	$17.95	
French Holiday Homes	Edition 1	$17.95	
	Total $		

Shipping in the continental USA: $3.95 for one book, $4.95 for two books, $5.95 for three or more books. Outside continental USA, call (800) 243-0495 for prices. For delivery to AK, CA, CO, CT, FL, GA, IL, IN, KS, MI, MN, MO, NE, NM, NC, OK, SC, TN, TX, VA, and WA, please add appropriate sales tax.

Please make checks payable to: The Globe Pequot Press   Total $

To order by phone with MasterCard or Visa: (800) 243-0495, 9am to 5pm EST; by fax: (800) 820-2329, 24 hours; through our web site: **www.globe-pequot.com**; or by mail: The Globe Pequot Press, P.O. Box 480, Guilford, CT 06437

Date _____

Name _____

Address _____

Town _____

State _____

Zip code _____

Tel _____

Fax _____

BOOKING FORM

À l'attention de:
To:
_____

Date:
_____

Madame, Monsieur
Veuillez faire la réservation suivante au nom de:
Please make the following booking for (name):

_____

Pour	*nuit(s)*	*Arrivée le jour:*	*mois*	*année*
For	night(s)	Arriving: day	month	year
		Départ le jour:	*mois*	*année*
		Leaving: day	month	year

Si possible, nous aimerions   *chambres, disposées comme suit:*
We would like   rooms, arranged as follows

À grand lit	*À lits jumeaux*	
Double bed	Twin beds	
Pour trois	*À un lit simple*	
Triple	Single	
Suite	*Appartement*	*ou autre*
Suite	Apartment	or other

Nous sommes accompagnés de   *enfant(s) âgé(s) de*   *ans.*
Avez-vous un/des lit(s) supplémentaire(s), un lit bébé; si oui, à quel prix?
We are travelling with   childern, aged   years. Please let us know
if you have an extra bed/extra beds/a cot and if so, at what price.

Notre chien/chat sera-t-il le bienvenu dans votre maison?
Si oui, y a-t-il un supplément à payer?
We are travelling with our dog/cat. Will it be welcome
in your house? If so, is there a supplement to pay?

Nous aimerions également réserver le dîner pour   *personnes.*
We would also like to book dinner for   people.

Veuillez nous envoyer la confirmation à l'adresse ci-dessous:
Please send confirmation to the following address:

Nom: Name:
_____

Adresse: Address:
_____

_____

Tel No: E-mail:
_____

Fax No:
_____

Guided visits of Paris gardens

The City of Paris Gardens Department offers guided visits in English and French of some 120 highly individual and interesting gardens.
Details from +33 (0)1 40 71 75 60.

Père Lachaise garden–cemetery, Boulevard de Ménilmontant (Metro Père Lachaise)
This former Jesuit garden, a place of grand trees and lush fertility, was made a public cemetery by Napoleon 200 years ago and the declarations of immortality have flocked ever since. It is, in effect, an open-air gallery of two centuries of funeral sculpture where visitors can wander among the mortal remains of the greatest musicians (Chopin, Rossini, Bizet), where some of France's undying poets have left bits of their souls among the monuments (Musset, Apollinaire, Nerval) and painters are remembered in marble (Ingres, Delacroix, Pissarro). Not to forget mainstream non-conformists such as Édith Piaf, Oscar Wilde and Jim Morrison.

Come for a contemplative stroll or a detailed explanation by a qualified guide of one or other of the cemetery's specific attractions.

Visits in English at 3pm on Saturdays in July and August.

Bagatelle, Bois de Boulogne
(Bus 43 from Gare St Lazare to Place de Bagatelle)
Renowned for its roses - old classics in a formal garden, hardy landscape roses in wilder settings - Bagatelle also has thousands of bulbs in spring and 130 clematis, 300 astonishing iris's and masses of peonies in early summer.

Individual visits € 5.70; special groups € 83 + € 24 for foreign languages or Sundays and bank holidays (2003 prices).

QUICK REFERENCE INDICES

Wheelchair   Places with facilities for people in wheelchairs but please check for your specific requirements when booking.

- 5 Washington
- 10 Bourg Tibourg
- 11 Victories
- 45 Le Clos Médicis
- 52 Clement
- 54 Buci
- 63 La Villa
- 80 Bosquet-Tour Eiffel
- 83 Tulipe
- 87 Frémiet
- 96 Régence Étoile
- 100 Villa Maillot
- 103 Flaubert
- 107 Lavoisier
- 114 Favart
- 116 Pulitzer

Garden – Patio   These places have gardens or patios where guests can sit.

- 12 Gilden Magenta
- 15 St Paul le Marais
- 18 Le Jeu de Paume
- 26 Les Gobelins
- 45 Le Clos Médicis
- 56 Aubusson
- 57 Nesle
- 60 Millésime
- 61 Hôtel des Marronniers
- 64 Danube
- 65 L'Hôtel
- 71 Varenne
- 83 Tulipe
- 97 Centre Ville Étoile
- 100 Villa Maillot
- 101 Résidence Impériale
- 102 Regent's Gardens
- 103 Flaubert
- 121 Terrass' Hotel

Architecture & Design   Places with particularly striking architectural or design features.

Old architecture and styles:
17th – 19th centuries

- 5 Washington
- 9 Saint Merry
- 18 Le Jeu de Paume
- 49 Louis II

QUICK REFERENCE INDICES

Interior Design   Traditional/contemporary

INDEX

INDEX

CONVERSION TABLE

Euro€	US$	£ Sterling
1	1.01	0.64
5	5.05	3.20
7	7.07	4.48
10	10.10	6.40
15	15.15	9.60
20	20.20	12.80
30	30.30	19.20
40	40.40	25.60
50	50.50	32.00

December 2002

EXPLANATION OF SYMBOLS

Treat each one as a guide rather than a statement of fact and check important points when booking.

Full and approved wheelchair facilities for at least one bedroom and bathroom and access to all ground-floor common areas.

Pets are welcome but may have to sleep in an outbuilding or your car. Check when booking.

Payment by cash or cheques only.

Licensed bar on the premises.

Modem connections available.

Lift installed. It may stop short of the top floor or start on the first floor.

The hotel has its own restaurant of a separately-managed restaurant next door.

Air conditioning in bedrooms. It may be a centrally-operated system or individual apparatus.

Meeting room available.